I0661861

William Selwyn

Cape carols and miscellaneous verses

William Selwyn

Cape carols and miscellaneous verses

ISBN/EAN: 9783337057329

Printed in Europe, USA, Canada, Australia, Japan

Cover: Foto ©Thomas Meinert / pixelio.de

More available books at **www.hansebooks.com**

AND

MISCELLANEOUS VERSES

BY

WILLIAM SELWYN. of Port Elizabet

"*From grave to gay, from lively to severe.*"—POPE.

All profits on the sale of these Poems will be handed to the Ladies' Benevolent Society of Port Elizabeth.

Cape Town:

ARGUS PRINTING AND PUBLISHING COMPANY, LIMITED.

1891.

PREFACE.

 HE "Stream of Song" in South Africa partakes of the character

of most of its rivers. Scanty in volume, it struggles along in

ERRATA.

PAGE.	LINE.	
50	1.	For " passion's " read " passions'."
81	1.	For " bleeding " read " pleading."
82	7.	For " with " chilling read " but " chilling.
85	13.	For " it's ' read " 'Tis."
92	10.	For " seedling " read " seedling.'
93	3.	For " toil to built " read " toil to build up."

and moral wastes with grace and gladness.

WILLIAM SELWYN.

Port Elizabeth, February 1891.

PREFACE.

THE "Stream of Song" in South Africa partakes of the character of most of its rivers. Scanty in volume, it struggles along in an obscure channel, amid dreary and untuneful surroundings, only glancing in the sunlight and beautifying the scene at widely separated intervals. The author of the following fugitive verses—written during some pleasant hours of relaxation in a long and busy official life—hence gathers hope that his fellow colonists will not bury his small tributary beneath the arid sands of unappreciative sneers and carping criticisms; but that with a generous allowance for circumstances, they will rather clear its course, and hail it as possibly a harbinger of more powerful and diffusive affluents, which in the glorious future now dawning on our adopted country will, it is hoped, bear their part in spreading its mental and moral wastes with grace and gladness.

WILLIAM SELWYN.

Port Elizabeth, February 1891.

SONNET

TO THE

Memory of FRANCIS TUDHOPE, Esq.,

FOR MANY YEARS

PRINCIPAL OF THE GRAHAM'S TOWN GOVERNMENT SCHOOL,

DIED 27TH AUGUST, 1870.

GUIDE of my youth! in memory's holiest shrine
    Thy sacred image stands love-garlanded ;
    Thy noble life fills up a glowing line
Of the universal hymn by angels led.
'Tis meet that I inscribe my rhymes to thee,
Whose kindly hand first ope'd the fount of song ;
What thoughts may wing their halting melody,
What longings after good, what scorn of wrong,
What worthy aspirations lend their fires,—
They're all but imprints from thy loving heart.
My timorous muse to no vain height aspires,
She loves to gaze on Truth's inspiring chart ;
Let worldlings scout! bright Fancy greets with joy
The smile that cheered the struggles of the boy.

INDEX.

viii

THE RHYME OF THE OX-WAGON.

A MODEST PENDANT TO PRINGLE'S " AFAR IN THE DESERT."

AWAY with the cynic who ceaselessly sighs
    For some new-fangled bauble, some novel surprise;
Give me the heart that with generous glow
Lights up the friendships of long long ago.
Green be the mem'ries of pleasure gone by
When youth filled the cup, and no care breathed a sigh.
Fain would I weave into light-tripping rhyme
The frolicksome joys of the good olden time,
Ere our evergreen forests, and still wilds were scared
    By the ear-piercing screech of the Railway Dragon ;
And a thousand long miles were triumphantly dared
    'Neath the cosy white tent of a good Ox-wagon.

B

How jocund the shout of the old driver, Jan,

With his grimy felt hat and his jacket of tan :

The crack of his whip waking echoes around,

While the startled bush-buck clears the path with a bound.

As the tall forest trees bend their heads 'neath the breeze,

So our team breasts the steep with a labouring wheeze ;

Then down the long slope in a sinuous race

They scamper along at a bullock's best pace ;

" Wo-haa ! " shouts the driver. " Wo-haa ! " for the sake

    Of the small Tottie leader with scarcely a rag on,

Who capers and hoots, gamely striving to break

    The headlong descent of the good Ox-wagon.

How grateful the halt near the bush-margined stream

Where " uitspanned," our hungry and sweltering team

Lave their hot dusty hoofs, and with heads bending low,

Drink the nectar that Adam imbibed long ago.

Old Jan and the Tot gather sticks for a fire

To prepare the hot coffee (what liquor ranks higher?)

And the lush " carbonaitje,"[1] whose tender delight

To the palate still clings though you've dainties in sight

With the biscuits and " biltong "[2] we finish our feast;

   (Perhaps we may take a small sip from the flagon)

Then join in the chase of a runaway beast

   Who freedom prefers to the good Ox-wagon.

The " inspanning " finished Jack shoulders his rifle ;

His longing for venison all gentle thoughts stifle.

Peeping Bob is intent upon catching things horrid ;

While Bill who confesses to sympathies florid

Gathers trophies galore, of old Cape's blossomed splendour,

While a grateful thought leaps to the bountiful Sender.

Such our innocent joys while our caravan rumbles

At three miles an hour, to the trysting at " Bumbles."

---

[1] " Carbonaitje."—The Colonial designation of a piece of mutton roasted on a forked stick or live coals, in the absence of the more civilized gridiron.

[2] " Biltong."—Pieces of meat, usually venison, salted and dried in the sun and eaten raw.

4

Fain would I tell of our jollity there,

But time gently warns me to tackle the drag on ;

So I leave you to picture our sumptuous fare

While we drank " Happy days with a good Ox-wagon."

Well ! what have we gained by our *steaming* hot hurry

But time-tables, tariffs, debts, drivings and worry ?

We've lost half an hour by a trick that looks dirty ;

Old five-o'clock reads as the modern " four-thirty,"[1]

On a " sliding scale " lately we've slid fast enough,

Though the " ways " of that slide have been terribly rough.[2]

---

[1] "Old five o'clock reads as the modern four-thirty."—The longitude of Port Elizabeth is about 7½ degrees East of that of the Cape Observatory giving nearly half an hour difference between railway time and local time, which at the first introduction of railways was a source of intense puzzlement to poor benighted Cape Colonists.

[2] On a "sliding scale" lately we've slid fast enough.—The period some years before and after the date of this composition was one of great commercial depression and agricultural distress. Great pressure was brought to bear upon the Railway Department by the Cape Town merchants to induce the adoption of a "sliding scale" for reducing the railway rates in proportion to the distance travelled, the object being to "handicap" Port Elizabeth in its competition for the Kimberley trade.

Our railways and war's weary wasting alarms

Have ravaged our profits, and mortgaged our farms ;

Our wool, wine, and wisdom are not in " high feather ;"

    But, up with the whipstick ! Bend Hope's sunny flag on !

" Give a long pull, a strong pull, a pull altogether,"

    And cheers shall yet ring from the old Cape wagon.

THE VICTORIA FALLS ON THE ZAMBEZI.

WRITTEN AFTER READING DR. EMIL HOLUB'S DESCRIPTION.

YON fleecy cloud in convolutions piled,
    Proclaims an ever-seething caldron, where
Zambezi hurls her gathered rills and streams
In thundering torrents o'er "Victoria Falls,"
Whose far off sound like coming simoon blast
Or groans from Etna's close-pent liquid fires
Enwraps the soul in dread and solemn awe.
    Impelled by somewhat of the fateful lure
That draws the bush-dove to its conscious doom
Where hooded cobra gaping waits its fall,
In curious fear, I thread the forest maze,
Alone, unguided, save by a frisking troop
Of graceful zebras, whose enquiring eyes
Ask why this trespass on their wild doman.

" The voice of many waters " nearer swells

Till Nature seems to hold her breath in fear.

Still on the track of my unconscious guides

I clear at length the chilling forest shade

And climb a rising ground, when "all at once,"

Old Afric's grand primeval marvel starts

In majesty appalling on the sight.

Rapt, dazed, and faint, I sink upon the turf ;

The heart's full tide responds in labouring throbs

To the torrent's undistinguishable roar,

While humbled thought can only eddy round

The deprecating cry, " Lord what is man

That Thou of him shouldst ever mindful be ?"

And yet methinks these fearless flowers that raise

Their heads around the spot on which I sit,

Proclaim alike His mindfulness and love.

My wildered sense composed by needful rest,

With soul attuned and raptured eye, I drink

In luscious draughts the beauty of the scene.

A gentle breeze like fairy's magic wand

Dispels the misty shroud that overhangs

Bright palm-clad isles, whose glowing pictures lie

Embosomed on the verdure-margined stream

That winds its way from yonder azure hills,

Smooth and pellucid as the sea of glass

In John's apocalyptic vision seen.

With confluent force it nears the awful brink

And seems to pause in terror ere it plunge

In flashing cascades o'er the dizzy steep.

Serrated rocks in grim array diffuse

A thousand glancing jets and foaming wreaths

That midway shrink in vapour from the abyss.

Yonder, a giant stream's resistless tide,

Like Balaclava's gallant death-doomed host,

With scorn-curled edges dares the yawning gulf

Whose seething surge with tremor thrills the earth.

Fit emblems of the desolating strife

That through long ages past has ruthless rolled

O'er hills and plains whence thou, Zambezi fair,

Hast gathered wide thy tributary streams.

But lo ! the westering sun's resplendent glow

Has caught the hovering fleecy cloud, and flung

A bow with hues of heaven athwart the scene.

In tints ineffable it seems to join

The soft translucent sky, and form a way

For angel visitants, with messages

Of Peace, and Hope, for Afric's swarthy sons.

THE OLD SETTLER'S REMINISCENCES.

———

The driver cracked his whip and drove away leaving us to our reflections.
My wife sat down on one box and I on another; the beautiful blue
sky was above us and the green grass beneath our feet."—

REV. WILLIAM SHAW

———

COME take my arm my dear old wife
　　To yonder shady seat,
And let us talk of by-gone life
　　So bitter and so sweet,
Since first we sat with children four
On boxes filled with all our store,
The bright blue sky above our heads
And green grass 'neath our feet.

Let us recall the anxious day
　　When drenched with surf we trod
The sandy shore of Algoa Bay,
　　With thankful hearts to God

For safe deliverance from the deep,

In whose dark bed so many sleep,

For bright blue sky above our heads

And firm earth 'neath our feet.

Let mem'ry paint the chilling hush,

 The tremulous alarms,

While slow we toiled through Addo bush—

 A baby in your arms—

The wolf's deep howl, the night hawk's scream,

The evening " uitspan " near a stream ;

Clear starry skies still glowed o'erhead

Though rough roads galled our feet.

Our hearts still feel the grateful thrill

 As sod by sod up-piled,

Our rush-thatched cottage 'neath the hill

 With welcome shelter smiled ;

Our little ones like " spring-boks " free

The crowning hailed with shouts of glee,

While bright blue sky beamed high o'erhead
And flowers bloomed round our feet.

Can aught obliterate the scene
   When War like prairie foam
Swept all our cattle from the green
   And fired our cottage home?
In trembling fear and anguish sore
We saw the wreck of all our store,
Blue sky was still our shield o'erhead
Though sharp thorns pierced our feet.

Again we toiled, and God hath sped
   With solace for our fears;
Glad health and peace their blooms have shed
   On our declining years.
Our sons will sail on Fortune's wave
When soft we slumber in the grave;
May bright sky canopy their heads
When grass grows *o'er* our feet.

THE GOLD DIGGERS.

"Two men between Waterberg and Limpopo were found dead in the
"veldt" with their gold beside them."—"Port Elizabeth Telegraph."

ᘺITH hopes elate two diggers tough
    Set forth at Fortune's call
O'er parched karoo and mountains rough
    To mines beyond the Vaal ;
At night 'mid Nature's soothing hush
They soundly slept beneath a bush,
    Their picks and spades beside them.

With visions fair of gold up piled
    They cheered the dreary way,
And bright with loving welcomes smiled
    A glad returning day.
Sworn brothers they through good and ill,
One purse they'd share as one repel
    What dangers might betide them.

Foot-sore and faint at length they gain

 The Eldorado bleak.

Long months 'mid weariness and pain

 The glitt'ring gold they seek.

At night their little store concealed

From prowlers rough who throng the field,

 They sleep with guns beside them.

At length their modest hopes complete

 They speed their homeward track,

But no glad wife shall loving greet

 Nor child shout " welcome back."

From far horizon's hazy belt

[1]" Aasvogels" scan the scorching " veldt"[2]

 Where they *die*—their gold beside them.

---

[1]" Aasvogels."—The Colonial designation of the common vulture. Th enormous distance from which these scavengers scent carrion, or otherwise " spot " it, is almost incredible. On the death of an animal they seem to troop instinctively from all parts of the dim horizon to the spot, where they gorge themselves till perfectly unable to rise from the ground.

[2]" Veldt."—Open uncultivated country. Those lines were written in the early days of South African gold digging, before the discovery of the wonderfully rich fields of Johannesburg, in the " South African Republic."

AN ALGOA BAY SOUTH-EASTER.

"OF a' the airts the wind can blaw,"
 The one I love the least—
Depressing as a suit at law—
 Is an Algoa Bay South-East.
If maledictions deep and loud
Can pierce the louring murky shroud,
Whence Boreas blusters, cheeks a-blowed,
 He'll know himself "a beast."

His chill blast bears tic douloureux,
 The toothache and the mumps,
Rheumatic pains, and all the crew
 Of ills that gender dumps.
Your collar droops, your hat is grimy,
Your eyes are bleared, your nose is rimy,
Life's loosened harp-strings jar untimely,
 Your hopes are leaden lumps.

The poets sing of " balmy breezes,"

   But they're a long way off :

A Bay South-East gives birth to sneezes,

   And racking lung-sick cough.

The bending blue-gum's ragged tops

Proclaim the poisoned breath that lops

Their tender shoots, and leaves green crops

   A limp bedraggled scoff.

A blinding cloud of cutting sand

   Comes scudding down the street,

You're brought unwilling to a stand,

   Uncertain of your beat.

You seek a refuge in your den,

And find your paper, ink, and pen

Must be restored to use again

   By excavations neat.

Lo! South-East breakers forward sweep,

   Save where with thundering shock

They suddenly in mid-air leap

   To clear the Roman Rock.

They course before the driving blast

As if each feared to be the last

To charge the ships, whose mooring fast

   Each wave would fain unlock.

How lightly rides the jaunty " Sprite,"

   High on the surge's crest,

Right bravely she maintains a fight

   That knows no breathing rest.

Alas! yon ponderous foaming wave

Holds dread design to be her grave,

The taut chain snaps! what power can save

   The " Sprite" from Fate's behest?

c

Hold hard my boys, and port the helm "—

Now Heaven preserve the ship—

A broadside wave her decks o'erwhelm,

  She heels till bulwarks dip.

She rights again, and madly reels

To the sandy beach, where a requiem peals,

For many before who have ground their keels

  'Neath the lash of the South-East whip.

O may a blast from Vulcan's bellows

  Sweep Boreas into Hades,

The hushing place for blustering fellows,

  Where the loudest but a shade is.

But hold ! let justice be allowed—

From yonder gathering western cloud,

That bears inland a rainy shroud,

  His debt of ill repaid is.

THE ATTACK ON THE LAAGER.[1]

THE fires are put out, and the sentries are placed ;
   Thick darkness appalling has gathered around ;
The cattle are kraaled and the wagons well braced.
The herd with his gun lies asleep on the ground.

Nought is heard save the bark of the faithful watch dog,
Or the wolf's dismal howls that in distance expire ;
Nought is seen save the gleams through the darkness and fog
Of our thatch-covered homes and our haystacks on fire.

The Kaffirs are coming ! their war-cry's fierce yelling,
Discordant as cries of doomed spirits below ;
Away to your stations, all craven thoughts quelling,
No quarter expect from the merciless foe.

Give the women spare guns ; bid them tuck up their skirts,
Let each fill her " sakkie " with powder and ball ;
They'll load while we fire : keep at hand some old shirts,
To bandage the hurts of our men should they fall.

The conflict is ended 'tis morning once more,

See disclosed to the view the results of the fight ;

Lo ! grim Kaffir warriors bespattered with gore,

Still grasping their spears—'tis a horrible sight.

Despite our achievements they've captured our cattle,

Their dearly bought booty's concealed in the kloof,

But mount brother burghers again give them battle

Till courage rewarded regains every hoof.

[1] "Laager" is the colonial designation of an extemporized fortification composed of wagons drawn up in the form of a hollow square and braced together with thongs of raw hide (riemen), under cover of which the attacks of hordes of savages have often been repelled by mere handfuls of men during the many wars which in past days devastated the Eastern portion of the Colony.

THE PORT ELIZABETH PYRAMID.

The Pyramid which forms the subject of the following lines is the most prominent historical monument of Port Elizabeth. It stands on the brow of the hill overlooking Algoa Bay, in an open space known as the " Donkin Reserve." It is built of rough stone and is about 35 feet in height, each side of the base being about 25 feet. On its Western side a slate tablet is inserted exhibiting the following inscription :—

"Elizabeth Frances, Lady Donkin, eldest daughter of Dr. George Markham, Dean of York, died at Merat in Upper Hindostan, of a fever after seven days of illness, on the 21st August 1818, aged not quite 28 years. She left an infant in his seventh month too young to know the unequalled loss he had sustained, and a husband whose heart is still wrung by undiminished grief. He erected this Pyramid, August 1820."

On its Eastern side a similar tablet appears exhibiting the following.

"To the Memory of one of the most perfect of human beings who has given her name to the town below."

" Sermons in stones
And good in every thing,"—SHAPESPEARE.

I SEEK not with a weak and untuned lyre
To sound the praise of Cheop's mighty pile,
Where toiling myriads, higher and still higher,
In the dim past, beside the swirling Nile,

Heaped up those giant masses to the sky,

Upon whose hoary sides old Time's grim teeth

Have spent their force in vain. From task so high

My muse with trembling shrinks. If e'er a wreath

Should decorate her brow, 'twill twine 'mong themes

Of lowly sort. Be hers the touch that thrills

Heart's deepest chords. Be hers the light that beams

From Nature's restful face ; the love that fills

The Home with flowers of Eden's chastened bloom.

And surely this love-reared memorial pile,

To sacred dust enshrined in Indian tomb,

A theme congenial yields. The wordling's smile,

Incredulous, mayhap reveals the thought

That from rough stones no poet-flowers can rise

In gladdening bloom, no wisdom's lore be taught.

Erected here, perchance to tranquilize,

That "undiminished grief," whose darksome tide

For two long years had whelmed Sir Rufane's heart,

This Pyramid on Donkin's Hill, beside

The towering lighthouse stands ; and with rude art

Its sculptured tablets tell that she whose loss

The stricken husband mourned, a babe had left,

Too young to feel the orphan's bitter cross.

That earth in her recall had been bereft

Of one pure gem whose ray reflected heaven.

In touching tones, the simple record speaks

The fondness of a heart by anguish riven.

Methinks hot tears o'er-stream his haggard cheeks,

As memory mirrors her lov'd form to view.

And all her tender ministrations pour

In recollections, soft as evening dew.

The well-known voice now hushed for evermore.

Has left its echoes sighing through his heart

And as her faith and tranquil virtues rose

To vision clear, he sought but to impart

A brief epitome, that should disclose

All that she was to him, when on her scroll

This record he inscribed ; that all might know

That she was " one most perfect human soul,"
Whose name in fragrance marks the " town below."

When gloomy night her sable mantle spreads,
And storm-winds fill the seaman's heart with fear,
The lighthouse pours its placid ray, and sheds
A soft effulgence on this tribute dear.
The keeper's cottage, nestling low between
The lighthouse and the sombre monument,
Shares the mild radiance that o'erspreads a scene
Whose light appears with mystic shadows blent.

What sober thought may Faith's clear eye perceive
With Fancy's pictures fair to interweave?
Light from above reveals the rocks and shoals
Whose earth-born flashes shipwreck storm-toss'd souls.
Light from above illumes the smiling home ;
Light from above irradiates the tomb ;
'Light from above with sympathetic glow
O'ergilds the memories of our deepest woe.

A PATRIOTIC SONG.

————

LAND of serene and sunny skies,—
   Land of the lion and fleet gazelle ;
Land where the summer never dies,
   Cape of Good Hope ! we love thee well.

Land where the birds, in gorgeous plume ;
   Flit through the bush or their love song tell ;
Land where the flowers show Eden's bloom,
   Cape of Good Hope ! we love thee well.

Land where the hunter scours the plains,
   Free as a bird o'er the ocean's swell ;
Land of kind nature's soothing strains,
   Cape of Good Hope ! we love thee well.

Land where the grape and the orange grow
   Deep in yon cool sequestered dell ;
Land of the melon's luscious flow,
   Cape of Good Hope ! we love thee well.

Land where the fields of golden grain,

    Rich in their bounteous fruitage swell ;

Land of sleek herds in lengthened train,

    Cape of Good Hope ! we love thee well.

Land of a stalwart yeoman race, —

    Stern, but with hearts as true as a bell ;

Homely, but full of a kindly grace,

    Cape of Good Hope ! we love thee well.

Land of the dark Amakosa tall,

    Seeking release from the savage spell ;

Land where there's room and to spare for all,

    Cape of Good Hope ! we love thee well.

Land of Good Hope ! our prayer we raise,—

    May peace and plenty with thee dwell ;

Filling our hearts with grateful praise,

    For this bright land we love so well.

SONNET—THE MIMOSA.

I MARKED the young mimosa gaily dight
    With feathery foliage trembling in the breeze,
And tufts of golden flowers, whence drowsy bees,
Sweet-laden, hummed their unrestrained delight.
In after years the full-grown tree I passed ;
Its flowers and foliage gone, and in their stead
A crop of huge white thorns inspiring dread.
Father ! I pray that when life's blooms are cast,
And old age pours its snows upon my head,
Thy kindly hand, whose pruning skill adorns
" The trees of righteousness," may lop my thorns.
And may my roots, with dewy moisture fed,
Nourish a stem to which a child may come
And fearless gather drops of crystal gum.*

---

* A beautiful transparent gum exudes from the stem of the Mimosa of which colonial children are very fond.

THE EUPHORBIA.

GRACELESS and gaunt, the tall Euphorbia stands,
  With rigid arms like railway semaphores ;
Meet habitant of wild and desert lands,
Where vultures hover and the lion roars.

Its sickly florets spread a poisoned lure
Along the edges of its outstretched arms,
Where bees incautious gather juice impure,
Robbing their dainty store of all its charms.

No creeping tendril twines about its trunk,
No leafy shade falls round its rugged form ;
And fluttering songsters seem as if they shrunk
From boughs that lend no shelter from a storm.

In curious quest I pierce its dull green skin,
And mark white pearly drops like milk descend,
From whose vile taste, as from foul dregs of sin,
May kindly powers my palate e'er defend.

Nor less preserve me from a pride-sealed heart :

No soft ray piercing its self-shrouded blindness,

Whence flows in lieu of balm for sorrow's smart

A poisoned mock of " the milk of human kindness."

LEAD KINDLY LIGHT.

———

"A little earthen lamp, 1700 years old, was recently found in the East, which bore this inscription,—'The light of Christ shines for all.'—*Christian Express.* Dec. 1st, 1878.

———

THIS tiny lamp of fragile clay
    Once shed its faint and flick'ring ray,
  To cheer perchance some sage's hall :
Its light extinct, 'mid wreck it lies,
Through seventeen rolling centuries ;
Till disentombed, behold the truth,
Bright with the glow of pristine youth,
  "The light of Christ shines for us all !"

Hail glorious truth ! Thy music thrills
In echoes from Time's distant hills ;
  And still thy tones melodious fall.
Still may poor wand'rers lift their heads
To Him, whose face benignant sheds

Effulgent rays, to warm and cheer,

To waken hope, and banish fear ;

   " The light of Christ still shines for all ! "

The ice-built screens by bigots planned,—

As children's barriers in the sand,

   Dashed by the wild waves, sink and fall—

Melt in the beams from Jesus' face.

Vanish in mist and leave no trace :

Free as the breeze on mountain side,

Wide as the ocean's rolling tide,

   "The light of Christ still shines for all !"

Light, light for Afric's dusky throng ;

Light for the pris'ners held so long

   In superstition's blinding thrall ;

Light for the savage and the sage,

For smiling youth, and trembling age ;

Light for all sorrowing, sin-struck eyes,

That seek the pathway to the skies ;

   " The light of Christ still shines for all !"

"SHOULD IT BE ACCORDING TO THY MIND?"

Job xxxiv : 33

SHALL feeble, vain, presumptuous man
  Whose loftiest vision's but a span,
Impugn the vast mysterious plan
    By boundless wisdom laid?
Shall His omnipotent behest,
That thunders o'er wild ocean's breast,
Or lulls its surging waves to rest,
    By puny worms he stayed?

Shall man whose moments hurrying flee,
Like sparklets from a phosphor sea,
Prescribe to dread Eternity
    The laws of His domain?
Shall He who scans each circling pole,
And points the course the planets roll,
Seek wisdom from the darkling mole
    To guide the shining train?

Shall yon vast orb, whose kindling ray
Pours forth the universal day,
His glad, majestic progress stay ;
   Lest, haply, his bright beams
With light unwelcome should illume
The drowsy couch, and chide the gloom,
Of some voluptuous sluggard's room,
   And chase his idle dreams ?

Shall thirsty nature pant in vain
For showers of life-restoring rain ;
Shall desolation sweep the plain
   And beauty droop and die ;
Lest one bright drop's exultant spring
Should snap the spider's airy string,
Or dim, perchance, the golden wing
   Of some gay butterfly ?

Shall yon glad stream, whose sparkling tide

Spreads verdant beauty far and wide,

O'erleap its banks and turn aside,

   Or in the desert sink ;

Lest, haply, fraught with summer showers,

Its waves should ripple o'er the flowers

By children planted 'mid the bowers

   That tangle on its brink ?

No ! He, whose power with life endued

This glorious universe, pursued

In His design the highest good

   And happiness of all ;

And still, at His benign command,

Rich bounties gladden ev'ry land ;

And still He guides, with all-wise hand

   Each tenant of this ball.

O then, low-bending in the dust,

Cling to His Love, with child-like trust,

Believing that Omniscience must

    Know what for thee is best ;

Let resignation soothe thy cares ;

Let faith disperse thy gloomy fears ;

And God Himself shall dry thy tears

    In His eternal rest.

"LORD! WHAT IS MAN THAT THOU ART MINDFUL OF HIM!"

PANTING climbers to some barren height ;
　　Eager chasers of some phantom light ;
Emmets piling way-side domes of clay,
That, crushed to dust, the whirlwind sweeps away ;
　　Toilers vain, O Lord, are we.

Fluttering night-birds dazzled by the day ;
Way-worn travellers who have lost their way ;
Miners groping slowly in the gloom ;
Children sobbing round a mother's tomb :
　　Blind and helpless, Lord, are we.

Flow'rets drooping in the noon-tide sun ;
Autumn leaves descending one by one ;
Bubbles dancing on life's foaming wave ;
Shadowy spirits hurrying to the grave :
　　Frail and fleeting, Lord, are we.

Trembling sparklets of immortal fire ;

Infant songsters 'mid an angel choir ;

Tiny parts of one complex machine,

Guided by an architect unseen :

　　None unnoticed, Lord, by Thee.

Dewdrops glistening in a radiant love ;

Diamond sand-grains registered above ;

Separate nurslings of a Father's care,

That gently numbers every silken hair,

　　Weak and faithless though we be.

38

FAIR WORDS.

"Fair words gladden so many a heart."

LONGFELLOW.

LET no ill jest in laughter drest,
  Envenomed, cause a brother's smart ;
Court not the cynic's dark unrest ;
"Fair words gladden so many a heart."

The lark's bright song may not be strong,
But he skyward trills his little part ;
Be such our song—'twill not be long ;—
"Fair words gladden so many a heart."

As showers of rain on the thirsty plain
Exultant, make new beauties start ;
As soothing balm to the sufferer's pain
"Fair words gladden so many a heart."

Keep full in view the good and true ;
Let kindly deeds unsoiled by art,
In blessings bloom—your words though few
Will waken joy in so many a heart.

'Tis Wisdom's choice, to catch that voice
Whose gentle accents still impart,
The hope that bids the world rejoice,
In words that gladden so many a heart.

HYMN WRITTEN DURING THE ZULU WAR, 1879.

"And I, if I be lifted up from the earth will draw all men unto me."

O SAVIOUR, throned in peace above,
    Reveal Thy pierced side ;
And let the vision of Thy love
    Stay war's remorseless tide.

                Risen Saviour hear !

For white, for black alike didst Thou
    Low bow Thy fainting head ;
For all of ev'ry clime and hue
    Didst Thou Thy hearts' blood shed.

                Suffering Saviour hear !

Behold fair Afric's sunny lands,
    With reeking carnage strewed,
See God-made man with rigid hands
    In brother's blood imbrued ;

                Sorrowing Saviour hear

O hear the Briton's dying groan,
  The Zulu's piercing wail ;
O hear the famished orphan's moan,
  The widow's sobbing tale.

            Pitying Saviour hear !

In mercy stay the quiv'ring spear,
  Avert the death-winged ball ;
Pour balm for every scalding tear,
  And breathe Thy " Peace " o'er all.

            Mighty Saviour hear !

Draw weary warriors round Thy feet,
  By love's constraining cord ;
There let the scattered nations meet,
  And own Thee Sovereign Lord.

            Gracious Saviour hear !

HYMN FOR OPENING OF A PLACE OF WORSHIP.

O THOU whose regal presence fills
   The teeming earth and starry zone ;
Whose praise in ceaseless chorus swells
From myriad harps around Thy throne ;
   Thy servants' prayer,
   O deign to hear ;
And when Thou hear'st forgive.

The blessing of our father's God
With longing hearts we supplicate,
While far from home on Afric's sod
A house to Thee we consecrate.
   Thy servants' prayer,
   O deign to hear ;
And when Thou hear'st forgive

Long may the truth that frees the slave
Reverb'rate hence with clarion voice ;
Long may the Gospel's banner wave
Till Afric's savage wilds rejoice.

    Thy servant's prayer,

    O deign to hear ;

And when Thou hear'st forgive.

Here may the Saviour's boundless grace
With hope inspire the stricken soul ;
His gentle words breathe holy peace
When cares oppress and sorrows roll.

    Thy servants' prayer,

    O deign to hear ;

And when Thou hear'st forgive.

Here may the grateful song of praise
Gush forth from hearts attuned by love,
Hence may our prayers like incense rise
Returned in blessings from above.

Thy servants' prayer,

O deign to hear ;

And when Thou hear'st forgive.

When with glad shouts the topstone crowns

The temple reared by Jesu's grace,

May we be found as living stones

Each in his own appointed place.

Thy servants' prayer,

O deign to hear ;

And when Thou hear'st forgive.

The above hymn was composel for and sung at the opening of the
Presbyterian Church of Port Elizabeth, to most admirable and appropr
music composed by the Rev. H. H. Dugmore of Queenstown.

SYMPATHY.

" Rejoice with them that do rejoice and weep with them that weep."

ST. PAUL.

"God would seem to crave for the sympathy of His creatures"

BISHOP WEBB.

O FOR an angel's piercing ken to trace

    The interweaving threads that clasp in one

All beauteous things ; the seraph's ear, attuned

To catch the linked melodies that swell

From myriad hearts, and blend in cadences

Harmonious, round His mystic throne " who holds

" The waters in the hollow of His hand."

    This world is fraught with finest sympathies

That stretch their fond encircling tendrils out

To dull cold hearts.   The clinging clematis

With wind-waved kisses, vainly woos the gnarled

And bare mimosa, whence all life has fled,

And left but horrent thorns that pierce the hand.
So souls encrusted spurn the gentle touch
That wakes responsive life in love-lit breasts.

In teeming forms and still to varied ends
The hidden source of sympathetic streams
Its gushing treasure pours ; now dancing light
'Mid mimic rainbows from the fountain gay ;
Anon in shade it laves the brooklet's banks,
Or sweeps majestic through the thirsty plain.
The confluent wave that rolls with haughty force
In mild obedience to the placid moon,
Imprints each cranny of the rock-bound coast,
And laps with loving lips each tiny shell.
The self same spring whose gentle dews becloud
The sailor's eyes, the while his little child
Entwines its fingers in his shaggy beard,
Anon inrushing swells his storm-scarred breast,
And nerves him to the daring plunge that saves
A gasping brother from a swirling tomb.

O fount ineffable of gladdening light!
Thy Spirit pour, that fitly I may sing
Of that deep love that drew Thee from the skies
To seek the lost, and point their weary feet
To ways of happiness.   Homeless and poor
Thy thorn-strewed path was with the homeless ones,
Upon whose parchéd hearts Thy solace fell
As evening dews.   Thy soul outpoured itself
In deeds of soft beneficence and healing power ;
And at the last Thy human sympathy,
O'erleaping finite bounds, in darkness veiled
The sweet compassion of Thy Father's face.
O wondrous love ! All Nature's depths are moved !
Shall rugged rocks in trembling shivers break,
And no responsive echoes stir our souls ?
The blending clouds with sympathetic crash
In bellowing terrors ask, " Why *will* ye die" ?
The Spirit brooding o'er the universal scene,
In pleadings soft as sleeping infant's breath,

The question still repeats, " Why *will* ye die" ?

O may repentant sighs awake the strings

Of the great Æolian harp whose liquid tones

In swift ethereal undulations rise,

Until they touch the star-clad angels' lyres,

And fill all heaven with sympathetic song.

SHADOWS.

"In the shadow of thy wings will I rejoice." Ps. 63 : 7.

SHADOWS that soften the summer-day gleam ;

 Shadows that picture the cool, placid stream,

   Lend beauty to earth,

   And give bounteous birth

To fancies that furnish the poet's fair dream.

Beautiful shadows and shadows of fear ;

Shadows far flitting or lowering near,

   Lights intercepted,

   Broken, reflected,

Chequer our pathway from cradle to bier.

Shadows are we and we shadows pursue,

Heedlessly passing the solid and true ;

   Fame, pleasure, and wealth

   Aye vanish by stealth,

Leaving but mem'ries of sombrous hue.

Shadows illusive wake passion's wild rage

In the gambler's breast that embitter life's page ;

Shadows of terror,

Suffering and error

Envelop the drunkard from youth to chill age.

Wave shadows ruffle the glittering way,

Where dark ocean mirrors the rising moon's ray ;

So turmoil and sorrow,

And fears of to-morrow

Break on the pathway that leads to the day.

Shadows bedimming the little child's face,

Flit 'neath the glow of its mother's embrace ;

So care's shadows fly,

'Neath a beam from His eye,

Whose love pours new vigour for life's fainting race.

O, to repose 'neath His shadowing wing,

Rejoicing His goodness and mercy to sing ;

  Till, life's journey past,

  No sin-cloud shall cast

Its gloom o'er the glory that beams round our King.

ALWAYS THE SAME.

"There is a friend that sticketh closer than a brother." Prov. 18 : 24.
" Jesus Christ, the same yesterday, to-day, and for ever." Heb. 13 : 8.

WHEN friends with cold, averted gaze,
   Mark friendship's broken chain ;
When evil tongues or fancied wrongs
   Provoke their dark disdain ;
What healing balm the thought distils,
To soothe the wounded spirit's ills :
   " Our Master's aye the same."

No haughty frown upon His brow
   Repels the yearning heart ;
His sympathetic bosom feels
   Each keen though hidden smart.
Our mourned infirmities he knows,
He melts with all our sorrow's throes,
   For He is aye the same.

The same whose sad and loving look
  Reproached frail Peter's fears,
Whose pity marked his guilty blush
  And treasured up his tears.
" Lovest thou me ?" The question moved
Heart's deep, responsive chords, and proved
  The Master still the same.

The same who heard the wayworn pair,
  Heart-stricken by His fate,
While buried hopes and boding fears
  Dejected they relate.
His comforts fell like evening dew,
And ere He fled they raptured knew
  Their Master still the same.

To Bethany's dear home He comes
  At sorrowing friendship's call,
And blends His tears with drops which o'er
  A brother's memory fall.

As man He weeps ! but lo ! His voice,
" Lazarus, come forth," bids faith rejoice
   In God and man the same.

His love immutable as rocks
   Wide as the ocean flows ;
Nor death nor hell nor sin's rude shocks
   Disturb its calm repose.
Ho ! all ye heavy-laden, come ;
His breast affords a restful home.
   Our Master's aye the same.

CONSCIENCE.

T HE vagrant bee in search of honied store
   In devious flight explores the scented plain ;
Should distant clouds with gathering tempest lower,
Straight as a sun-beam home he flies again ;
And this his song as he skims the flowered karoo—
" Be to the best thou knowest ever true."

The seaman storm-tossed in his fragile bark,
When moon and stars reveal no kindly ray,
Escapes the perils of the midnight dark
By trustful yielding to the needle's sway ;
All danger past, it points this lesson too—
" Be to the best thou knowest ever true."

High on a fencèd throne in each man's breast
A stern Recorder sits with busy pen ;
Each thought and deed before him stands confessed,
No dark design eludes his piercing ken :
While clear o'erhead this precept gleams in view—
" Be to the best thou knowest ever true."

A smile benignant lights th' Recorder's face
The while some generous action he inscribes ;
Anon 'neath frowns his truthful fingers trace
Unholy deeds, deceits, and Godless gibes.
His glance, at pendent scourges wrapped in rue
Says,—" Be to the best thou knowest ever true."

With reckless scorn one meets that warning glance,
And higher piles transgression's grief-stored heap ;
Another reels through guilt's forbidden dance,
While subtle vapours dimly round him creep.
Vain shroud ! This God-writ rule still flashes through—
" Be to the best thou knowest ever true."

Wouldst thou escape the scathings of Remorse,
On bee-line path mark well thy journey's end :
Should baffling winds and gloom beset thy course,
Submit thy guidance to the wanderer's friend :
Through life's dark mazes firmly hold this clue—
" Be to the best thou knowest ever true."

LONGINGS.

GIVE me a childlike unquestioning trust
 In our Father's deep wisdom and pity,
Whose sifting is needed to cleanse from their dust
 Bright gems for the crystalline city.

Give me an eye to discern from afar,
 Through the storm-rack of evil and sorrow,
The soul-cheering gleam of Hope's rising day-star,
 Presaging a glorious morrow.

Give me a heart which reflects others' joy
 And weeps with a brother in anguish ;
The helping hand stretched with no sordid alloy
 To waifs who in life's battle languish.

Give me a memory mirroring clear
 Sweet tokens of friendship's affection,
While on its fair surface no hatreds appear
 To darken its placid reflection.

Give me a conscience awake to the call
    Of life's waiting monitress—Duty.
May work and prayer leave, when the night's shadows fall,
    Mementoes of grace-illumed beauty.

Give me a mind calm and patient that feels
    Its hold on Faith's anchor grow firmer,
And scorning the gauds vain philosophy deals,
    Lists nearing Eternity's murmur.

JUBILEE HYMN.

GREAT universal King,
 Whose praise archangels sing
  With lowly mien ;
Hear Thou from Afric's shore,
The prayers our hearts outpour,
That heav'ns o'erflowing store
  May bless our Queen.

Our grateful thanks we raise,
That bounteous length of days
  Has owned her sway ;
Long may her years extend,
Ere life's calm honoured end—
Let ripened joys attend
  Her autumn day.

We thank Thee for Thy grace,
Which through her life we trace
    By virtue's light ;
May he, her royal heir,
An equal blessing share,
When called by Thee to bear
    Her sceptre bright.

May Peace her empire bless,
May Truth and Righteousness
    Swell high their tide ;
May Afric's swarthy sons
Fling wide their spears and guns,
And drink the stream which runs
    Free from Thy side.

May counsels wise prevail
To lighten mis'rys tale
    And raise the mean ;

May Grace her radiance fling,

Till chimes in all hearts ring,

And freedmen's voices sing

God save the Queen !

The author has some pride in noting the fact that the above hymn was sung in three of the Churches of Port Elizabeth on the occasion of Her Majesty's Jubilee viz. " Trinity Episcopal Church, the Presbyterian Church and the Congregational Church.

"MEASURE FOR MEASURE."

"All things whatsoever ye would that men should do to you, do ye even so to them, for this is the law and the prophets."

FAINT glimpses of Eden still gladden our earth,
  In the lily's soft grace and the lamb's sportive mirth :
Eden's sun spreads its glory o'er calm evening skies,
Eden's innocence peeps from a little child's eyes ;
But what a more exquisite beauty would gleam
From the world of the heart, were this precept supreme—
" Be you unto others kind, gentle, and true,
In the measure you deem others should be to you."

Unheedful of volumes of legal lore dim,
Where right follows ghost-like some ethical whim ;
Come Fancy, truth-guided, thy pallet prepare
With tints from the rainbow, harmonious and fair ;

Picture scenes from a world where each heart is a shrine,

Whose calm recess treasures this canon divine —

" Be you unto others kind, gentle, and true,

In the measure you deem others should be to you."

The soldier's trade dies while his bravery springs,

To succour the fainting whose love round him clings ;

How blest an exchange for the halo of strife,

Where bullets pierce gateways for God-given life.

His carnage-strewn pathway to glory is barred,

By this peace-teaching maxim's beneficent guard—

" Be you unto others kind, gentle, and true,

In the measure you deem others should be to you."

No covetous longings embitter the breast,

Where duty's demands keep the balance at rest :

Detraction and slander slink backward in shame,

Where each, as his own, guards his brother's fair fame ;

No gay scandal-lovers with poisoned darts play,

No sneer curls the lip where this precept holds sway—

" Be you unto others kind, gentle, and true,

In the measure you deem others should be to you."

How fair is the banner by Commerce unfurled

To the cheery breeze spreading the wealth of the world,

Where none seeks to profit by ignorance rash,

Nor chicane robs a credulous neighbour of cash ;

What swarms of suspicions, deceptions, and lies,

Are crushed by this maxim like pestilent flies—

" Be you unto others kind, gentle, and true,

In the measure you deem others should be to you."

As the cloud-piercing Alps in calm majesty stand,

So in diginity rises the Senator band ;

No selfish aim deadens their sense of a wrong,

Or ruins the weak at the beck of the strong :

Their laws are built up for the help of the good,

On the rock, where for ages this statute has stood—

" Be you unto others kind, gentle, and true,

In the measure you deem others should be to you."

O Thou ! who from Palestine's mountains didst shower

Thy sayings of wisdom with soul-trancing power,

Enkindle desire in our self-centred hearts

For the halcyon joys thine approval imparts :

Bid our desert rebloom with the love-laden rose,

Whose perfumes this precept's soft breathings disclose—

" Be you unto others kind, gentle, and true,

In the measure you deem others should be to you."

ENOCH.

"And Enoch walked with God; and he was not, for God took him."
—Genesis v. 24.

MAN'S frail memorials of the sainted dead
    As flickering lights reveal the paths they trod ;
But steadfast gleams o'er distant ages shed,
Mark this fair record—"Enoch walked with God."

The patriarch's friend, who lent his aid to climb
Earth's rugged steeps, and blessed the fertile sod,
Has penned this entry on the scroll of time
To show that mankind yet may walk with God.

O glorious ending to a hallowed life
That left no earth-stain for Death's chastening rod,
No last regrets, no pain, no mortal strife !
He enters bliss—led by his father God.

Good Shepherd ! let our wandering way-worn feet

Be with Thy gospel's preparation shod ;

Cheer Thou our path with Thy communion sweet,

And give us entrance to a Home with God.

BEYOND.

"If I ascend up into heaven Thou are there; if I make my bed in hell behold Thou art there,"
"Even there shall Thy hand lead me and Thy right hand shall hold me."—Ps. cxxix. 8 and 10.

I GAZE upon a throbbing star
Whence sages say
The light that streamed in ages far
Now drops its ray.
My vision tracks that trembling string,
While thought revolves on baffled wing
To solve the souls deep questioning ;
" What lies beyond " ?

Proud science vainly strives to scan
Life's mysteries,
And bare the earth-bound frame of man
To curious eyes :

His viewless spirit wings its flight
Across a gulf where Faith's clear sight
Alone can pierce the infinite
    And dumb "beyond."

Father in Heaven ! where'er Thy seat
    Still unrevealed ;
Grant us to walk with steadfast feet
    Beneath Thy shield.
The universe is full of Thee ;
Thy kingdom's span—Eternity ;
Hold thou us up that we may see
    Thy light " beyond."

SPEAK OUT.

"Stand upright ; speak thy thought ; declare
The truth thou hast, that all may share."—LEWIS MORRIS.

JOYLESS the hidden mountain rill
    'Mid barren boulders creeps along,
But lo ! where verdure decks the hill
    It dances light to rippling song.

In vain the warning beacon light
    On wave-dashed headland towering stands,
If shrouding shutters bar the sight
    When doubt benumbs the pilot's hands.

The God-lit lamp within the breast
    Too oft is hid by pride's dark blind,
And angel thoughts self-centred rest
    That else had beamed to bless mankind.

O fellow traveller ! scorn the sneer

That fain would chill thy welling heart,

   Cherish the love that casts out fear,

And let thy voice that love impart.

Hast thou a soul that shrines the truth,

   A mind that spurns deceit and wrong,

A heart enfolding untold ruth

   For the weak down-trodden by the strong ?

" Stand upright ; speak thy thought ;" let none

   The outflow of thy lips restrain ;

The Master's voice rings clear, " Well done !"

   To each brave blow on Satan's chain.

ONE MEDIATOR.

"For there is one God and one Mediator between God and men, the man Christ Jesus." 1 Tim. 2 : 5.

THE temple veil was rent in twain
    When our great Mediator died ;
No altar smokes with victim slain
    Since scoffing soldiers pierced His side.

No longer priest nor holy saint
    In Mediatorial office stands ;
No more through types and shadows faint
    We learn our Father's clear commmands.

But still with mystic symbol spread
    Proud priestcraft shrouds His loving face ;
By monkish counsels darkly led
    Poor wanderers vainly seek His grace.

Of old when anxious mothers pressed
  Their babes beneath the Saviour's eye
And asked that His dear hand might rest
  Upon their heads with blessing high ;

The dark disciples' stern rebuke
  With rising wrath He listening heard ;
Each nestling in His arms He took
  And blessed it with a loving word.

And still He marks with angry frown
  Pretentious guardians of His grace,
Whose dogmas dim His regal crown
  And multiply a bigot race.

No God within his hands he needs
  Whose heart enshrines the Saviour's form,
Who childlike follows where He leads
  With loving trust through calm and storm.

Tell Him thy sorrows ; open wide

   The sin-closed windows of thy soul ;

His free love, poured in blissful tide,

   Will guide thee to a heavenly goal.

MUTUAL HELPFULNESS

TWO waving flowerets* close together grew,
    Exchanging kisses while the zephyr sighed ;
Alike they drank the cooling evening dew,
Or flaunted high their heads with graceful pride.
The while a hurtling storm its arrows flung,
Scathing alike tall tree and fragile flower,
In close embrace they round each other clung,
And by united strength withstood its power.
Thus Nature on her green and flowery dress
Writes lessons sweet of mutual helpfulness.

Not ours to know why storm-winds dash the flower,
Or why misfortunes on our pathway shower ;
But, as with meek and reverent eye we scan
The story of the good Samaritan,
Not flowers alone, but words divine impress
The duty clear of mutual helpfulness.

* Sparaxis pendula.

REST.

CLEAR through the hush of the Sabbath morn
  The loving Saviour's voice is borne,
In soothing tones to hearts world-worn,
    " Come unto me ye weary
    And I will give you rest."

From anxious fears and carking cares,
From struggles 'mid earth's daily snares,
From loads which life o'erburdened bears,
    " Come unto me ye weary
    And I will give you rest."

For vanished loved ones dost thou mourn?
Has Death thy heart-strings rudely torn?
Is thy lone path of sunshine shorn
    " Come unto me ye weary
    And I will give you rest."

In dark temptation's trying hour,

When passions' fires have proved their power,

And bitter tears repentant shower ;

    " Come unto me ye weary

    And I will give you rest."

When doubts like whelming surges roll ;

When hope forsakes the sinking soul ;

When darkness shrouds the longed-for goal,

    " Come unto me ye weary

    And I will give you rest."

In dull disease or rending pain,

When friendly balm is poured in vain ;

When days 'neath Death's deep shadows wane

    " Come unto me ye weary

    And I will give you rest."

O, Saviour ! Thou of all our woes

Hast meekly borne the keenest throes ;

May love our sin-bound hearts unclose

And let us—faint and weary—

Beneath thy wings find rest.

TRUST IN GOD.

"I only know that God is just
And every wrong shall die."—*Whittier.*

GIVE me to run with open face,
  A brow serene and clear,
And feet unswerving in the race
  Whose goal the angels cheer.
When doubts assail, may simple trust
  Ring out the firm reply,
"I only know that God is just,
  And every wrong shall die."

I cannot tell why evil reigns
  And sorrow spreads her pall,
Or why earth's pleasures, honours, gains,
  Drop not alike on all.

Faith bows before the Eternal " must,"

 Though dark the reason why ;

" I only know that God is just,

 And every wrong shall die."

As insects on some picture vast,

 We scan the dust in sight ;

The blended beauties forward cast

 We cannot see aright.

Until my vision, cleansed from dust,

 A wider range shall try,

I'll grasp the faith that " God is just

 And every wrong shall die."

PERSEVERANCE UNDER DISCOURAGEMENT.

Matthew xv: 21—22.

WITH trembling voice and bleeding hands
A Canaanitish woman stands,

Allured by Christ's benignity:

Her troubled daughter's wild despair

Draws forth the agonizing prayer

"O Son of David, succour me."

His pity breathes a si'ent sigh,

But yet her suit wakes no reply,

While dark disciples scornful frown:

"Send her away," they sternly say,

"Let not her cries disturb our way.

"Why heed a Gentile's idle moan?"

G

Still as she scans the Saviour's face,

Her faith discerns compassion's trace,

      Encouraging her mournful plea :

" My daughter ! O my daughter heal !

" Her vexèd spirit's chain unseal!

      " O Son of David, succour me."

With eyes suffused, with chilling speech,

He speaks the language bigots teach,

      To show the grace of a Gentile heart :

" I cannot take the children's bread

" To feed the dogs," He slowly said ;

      " With Jews the Gentile's have no part."

Transported by a mother's love,

With strong-winged faith that soared above

      The scorn which uncouth Gentiles bear ;

Drawn by the Healer's pitying eyes

"Truth Lord," with meekness she replies,

      " But dogs the fallen morsels share."

Like the hidden spring from Horeb's rock

That gushed for Moses' fainting flock

    O'er-flowing love now thrills His voice ;

" Great is thy faith, O woman true !

" E'en as *thou wilt,* be it to you,

    " Thy prayer is heard, go and rejoice."

84

IN TIME OF TROUBLE.

"I was dumb: I opened not my mouth, because Thou didst it."—
Ps. xxxix, 3.

"TOO hard the lesson, gracious Lord,"
  The voice of nature moans.
Affliction strikes her wailing chord,
  We cannot hush its tones.
Yet there is balm to soothe our smart,
  It calms the weary aching heart
To know "Thou didst it."

Our wayward wills would choose the rod
  Thy chastening hand shall wield ;
Our loved one laid beneath the sod
  With rebel hearts we yield.
Help us to raise our earth-bound eyes,
  And see e'en this bereavement wise
Because "Thou didst it."

Not willingly dost Thou distress,

   Or grieve the sons of men,

And soon with yearning tenderness

   Thy smile breaks forth again.

Whate'er the stroke that wrings our woe,

   Low at Thy footstool may we know

In love "Thou didst it."

The sobbing child with conquered will

   Clings closer to the breast,

So, Father, Thou dost chasten till

   We fly to Thee for rest.

O teach Thou us when sorrows swell

   From childlike hearts to say " 'its well,"

Because "Thou didst it."

ENDURING SONG.

"This is sure,
"The song which longest shall endure
"Is simple, sweet, and pure."

LEWIS MORRIS.

SIMPLE as the lark's soft note

That lures its fledglings to the sky ;

Sweet as the chords that trembling float,

While zephyrs through the forest sigh ;

Pure as the rills from sunny hills,

Whence cascades leap with joyous thrills ;

Such is the song

That dureth long :

"Simple, sweet, and pure."

Simple as the evening prayer

By children lisped at a mother's knee ;

Sweet as the face of the angel there

Who bends in listening sympathy ;

Pure as that angel's whispered dreams
Which light the face with happy gleams ;
     Such is the song
      That dureth long :
" Simple, sweet, and pure."

Simple as the words that fell
In parables from lips divine ;
Sweet as the touching tones that swell
From His last hymn's low plaintive line ;
Pure as the sigh that bore on high
A prayer for the scoffers lingering nigh ;
     O may our song
      Such strains prolong—
Aye, " Simple, sweet, and pure."

ONWARD AND UPWARD.

"Find in loss a gain to match."
TENNYSON'S "In Memoriam."

I QUESTIONED the field of luxuriant grain
That billowed its breast to the redolent wind,
If aught were purloined from the harvester's gain
By the envious weeds that its stalks interwined.

With a rustle of conscious pride
The bountiful grain replied ;
'When my roots were young and tender,
And my stalks were green and slender,
The wildering weeds despoiled me of sun,
And drank up my share of the softening dew ;
But stoutly I've conquered them one by one
By strivings aye upward, unflinching and true.
And now when the storm-breezes ruthlessly blow,
And thunder-cloud torrents would lay my head low ;

The spoilers unwittingly lend me their aid

To face the rude blast, till my bounties are laid

In the garner at rest.   The weeds are then burned,

And their refuse uprising in wheat is returned.

I questioned the river that gleamed through the plain

With verdure deep-margined in limpid repose,

If the dark rocky ridges that traversed its train

Impeding its flow, waked disconsolate throes.

  The river in conscious pride

  To my question thus replied ;

  ' The rocks but serve to raise my bed

  And wider still my bounties spread.

When cloud-treasures tumble, majestic I sweep ;

O'er the arrogant blocks I exultingly leap ;

I speed on my course bearing joy through the waste ;

For deeds of emprize by resistance I'm braced ;

So I dash through the gorge where in impotent wrath

The dark frowning cliffs thunder rocks in my path ;

Then softly I spread o'er a smiling expanse
On whose billowy breast stately argosies dance ;
Then onward, still onward, rejoicing I roam,
Till I'm lost in the depths of my grand ocean home.'

I questioned the Teacher whose noble emprize
Was to light wand'ring souls on their track to the tomb,
And tune their sad harps to the songs of the skies,
If the sneer of the wordling diffused aught of gloom.
    The Teacher boldly thus replied ;
    ' With Jesus' banner for my guide,
    The scorner's laugh, the worldling's sneer,
    Pass harmless as an infant's fear.
The Master's clear plaudit " Good servant well done,"
Is my beacon ahead, glancing bright in the sun.
The weeds may entangle, the rocks may impede,
But daily His manna gives strength for my need ;
So I joyfully strive Zion's songs to inspire ;
In hamlet and hut I light prayer's altar-fire.

While " Hope springs exultant," that I by His grace

With my head jewel-crowned, and His light on my face,

Shall present my glad flock at the high court of heaven

Saying " Here, Lord, are those whom to me Thou hast

given."

WAITING.

"In quietness and in confidence shall be your strength."

ISAIAH.

O FOR that faith—that deep repose—
That clasps the thought, "*My Father knows.*"
O for the strength to do and dare,
Nor less, His call to waiting bear,
Content to follow Duty's lead,
And unrepining sow the seed.

As little children plant and sow,
And, ere the tender rootlets grow,
Impatient of the dull delay
Dig up the seeding in a day;
So we reject Hope's cheering lute
Because our saplings bear no fruit.

The fluttering songsters of the woods,

In anxious care for future broods,

Toil to built their little nests:

True to their Guider's high behests,

The pairs by turns, then " sit " in state ;

They've learned " to labour and to wait."

The rugged rocks and silent shore

Wait till the waves their gladness pour ;

The deep blue hills in solemn show

Wait for the morning's ruddy glow.

So may our souls in lowly form

Wait for His " Peace " above the storm.

THE GRAVE OF WILLIAM KOYI, KAFFIR EVANGELIST.

———

THE jungle may close o'er the desolate grave
   Of the Kaffir evangelist, humble and brave ;
No record in stone marks his place 'neath the sod,
But precious his dust in the sight of his God.

The voice of the Master, whose footsteps he traced,
Shall summon that dust from the wild lonesome waste ;
The records of Heaven hold the scroll of his fame,
And high among heroes stands Koyi's fair name.

Yea ! even on earth his " remembrance " is sure,
For the work of the righteous for aye shall endure ;
His faithful words spoken, his loving deeds done,
Shall blossom and bud while the long ages run.

SONNET

On the Jubilee of the Missionary career of the Rev
Richard Birt of Peelton.

HOW dim the splendour of the blazoned shield,
　Beside the halo caught from fifty years
Of patient toil, bedewed with silent tears
In some lone corner of the Master's field.
　And such the light, O venerable Birt,
Whose hallowed radiance decks thy silvered brow;
Bravely hast thou redeemed thy early vow
　And taught the darkling savage, pride-begirt,
To yield with heart subdued, and aspect mild,
　His willing tribute at thy Master's feet.
O glorious conquest! Afric's desert wild
　Lifts joyous hymns thy Jubilee to greet;
Prelude of songs from angel choir when thou
With thy saved flock before the Throne shall bow.

TO THE SOUTHERN CROSS.

HAIL! star-studded sign of the Christian's trust,
    From this glorious cerulean canopy gazing;
Thy twinkling gems culled from Heaven's diamond dust,
Seal the rock-founded promise of Afric's upraising.

Through long vanished yesterdays, changeless and calm,
Thy form has been mirrored on clear hidden lakes;
A pledge that the Son of Man's cross-purchased balm
Shall yet spread like oil where the savage tide breaks.

Untold generations of barbarous men,
Whose war plumes have glinted o'er mountain and plain;
As spectres have passed 'neath thy far-reaching ken,
Desolation and misery marking their train.

We cling to the hope which the promise inspires,
That the Cross shall yet gleam o'er the war-trampled sod;
We hail the first glow of the glad altar fires,
Where the Ethiop "stretches his hands unto God."

TO A BRANDY CASK.

FREE of the Exciseman's stern control,
    From the favoured West you gaily roll
To the land of the swarthy sons of Ham,
Who, lured by Cape Smoke's potent charms ;
Cluster around in ant-like swarms,
Each throat agape for a fiery dram.

The gathered "tickeys"[1] freely flow,
While "soupies"[2] set the brains aglow
And light up passions' baleful fires ;
Give, give, they cry, with eager yells,
Till an empty pouch the failure tells
Of the spring that slakes their wild desires.

Foul, ribald taunts wake flashing rage,
Till whirling "kerries"[3] solve the gage ;

And drunken warriors senseless sprawl,

Or staggering wide across the " veldt,"

They sink in death while fierce storms pelt,

And hungry wolves gloat o'er their fall.

All hail, Cape Smoke ! whose potent streams

Sweep " Native troubles" off like dreams,

Which squandered millions failed to do ;

The Native warrior keeps his gun,[4]

But let your barrel's free-tap run,

'Twill clear ere long the savage crew.

[1] " Tickeys," Three-penny pieces
[2] " Soupies " Three-penny drams
[3] " Kerries " Knobbed sticks

[4] The Colony spent between three and four millions in a war for the purpose of disarming the Basutos and—failed.

OUR "BRIDGE OF SIGHS."

"Still for all slips of hers,
One of Eve's family—
Wipe those poor lips of hers
Oozing so clammily."

Thomas Hood.

FULL length in a gutter
  A stalwart form lies,
With an ebony skin
  And brandy-glazed eyes.
From a gash in his head
  To the pitiless stones,
Drop by drop falls the blood,
  While faintly he moans.
His clothing is tattered,
  His dark breast is bare,
With foulness bespattered
  He poisons the air.

Policemen, deep loathing,

    Fling the wretch in a cart,

Unheeding his moaning,

    Or his gaping wound's smart.

Proud " Child of the Ages !"

    Christ's mark on thy brow

To whom wisdom's pages

    Teach care for the low ;

See the fruit of thy work

    At Mammon's behest !

Does no pity lurk

    In thy pelf-hardened breast ?

Behold here a creature,

    In God's image made,

Erst in soul and in feature

    As thine equal arrayed.

These red drops abhorrent,

That sprinkle the stones,

Are pure as the torrent

Thy sordid heart owns.

O'er yonder blue mountains

His fathers roamed free,

Nor lost at their fountains

Man's high dignity.

Not dead, the old spirit,

Though crushed below zero ;

Who denies *him* the merit

That crowns the true hero,

Who when a scorched host

Were dying *en masse*,

Held his life at no cost

To rescue his " baas ?"*

---

* At the great fire in De Beer's Diamond Mine, in which more than 150 miners perished, natives repeatedly imperilled their own lives to save those of their white overseers.

Dost thou for foul gain
  The unwary ensnare ;
And say with cursed Cain—
  " He is not in my care ?"
Thy canting prayer dies
  " To be kept from temptation,"
Whilst thou mockest the skies
  With Moloch's libation.

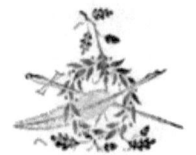

AN APPEAL.

"Two dead bodies of Natives, found, one on Saturday in the De Beer's location and one on Sunday morning near Poole's location, were examined on Monday last by the District Surgeon of Kimberley. Neither of the corpses bore any mark of violence, and the examination proved that death in each case resulted from *natural causes—Drink !"—E. P. Herald*, 7th October, 1887.

WAKE, sons of Afric, wake !

    For filthy lucre's sake

The tapster opens wide his diabolic den ;

    To prompt your potions deep

    He sells his poison cheap,

Till soul and senses steeped, ye sink, no longer men.

    Wake, sons of Afric, wake !

    Bid brandy-venders quake

Beneath the scornful glance that gleamed from sires of old ;

    Arise ye warrior's sons,

    Ye've dared the white man's guns,

And will ye now like slugs, prone 'neath his casks be rolled ?

Wake, sons of Afric, wake !

The drunkard's fetters break ;

Dash down the fiery cup that steals away your brains :

Loud let your war-cry swell,

And Heaven's glad plaudits tell

That swart men can be free from *Drink's* enslaving chains.

Wake, sons of Afric, wake !

Your friends' oppressed hearts ache ;

They bow their heads in grief, and mourn o'er labours vain ;

The scoffer's heartless breath

Sports o'er the " Native's" death ;

Close up your ranks, and swear, " *Drink shall no longer reign.*"

HYMN FOR THE TIMES.*

When the enemy shall come in like a flood the Spirit of the Lord shall lift up a standard against him. Is : 59. 19.

LIFT up Thy standard gracious Lord
    On Afric's mountains high,
Where sunk 'neath lusts by heaven abhorred
    Behold ! the people die.

Decrees unrighteous have gone forth
    Enlarging Satan's spoils,
Dark shadows hide Thy Gospel's worth
    While Christians spread his toils.

---

* The applicability of the above " Hymn for the Times" will be gathered from the following extracts from the "charge" of the Bishop of Cape Town at the opening of the eighth synod of the Diocese of Cape Town in September 1887.

"The principal hindrances to Church progress which are reported to me are ignorance and a low standard of morality amongst our people, with the inevitable accompaniment of the shockingly prevalent vice of intemperance." "And here I cannot omit to utter in the strongest terms I am capable of using my vehement protest against the action of our legislature

A dire intoxicating draught

   Is poured for shameful gain,

And struggling souls from Hope's frail raft

   In frenzed crowds are slain.

" Am I my brother's keeper," say

   Our rulers by their laws ;

While dusky suppliants, vainly pray

   For aid in virtue's cause.

Lift up thy standard mighty Lord

   Arrest sin's whelming tide ;

Raise up the drunkard by Thy word

   For whom the Saviour died.

in the last two sessions, first in repealing the Excise duty and secondly in removing the restrictions against the sale of liquors to the native races within certain defined areas in the Eastern part of the Colony." " If the native races were acknowledged to be the natural enemy of the white man, and if the great aim of the latter were to exterminate the former it is difficult to see what more successful action could be taken than that which has been taken by the legislature in the last few years. The natives even pray us to withdraw an almost irresistible temptation from them ; and our reply is to make brandy cheaper and to remove those restrictions to their obtaining it which have previously existed."

Let Mammon fall and heaven-born light
  Our rulers' minds unclose,
Make them the pillars of the right
  A terror to its foes.

SONNET

ON THE REV. R. TEMPLETON, PRINCIPAL OF THE UNDENOMI-
NATIONAL SCHOOL GRAHAM'S TOWN, WHO DIED IN THE
ZUURBERG FOREST, JANUARY 1886.

————

BY winding paths amid the tangled woods,

    That skirt the deep-kloofed Zuurberg hill,

A lately wedded pair meand'ring fill

Their cup of tender joy. The peace that broods

O'er Nature's tranquil face reflected shines

From loving eyes, as they in converse sweet

Plot out a rose-fringed path with prudence meet,

And mark with glowing hearts its " pleasant lines."

Mysterious are Thy ways great King of saints !

In sudden fear they, wildered, strive to thread

Their homeward track, when lo ! the husband faints

And silent sinks. His spouse with awful dread

Alone the wild maze dares in search of aid.

In vain ! The Teacher " sleepeth " in the shade.

SONNET

In Memoriam Martin Human, M.D., who died at sea March, 1886.

———

HUMAN ! well-named ! how oft have thy rare skill
    And " Human " kindness baffled Death's swift dart ;

Vengeful, he now has struck at thy great heart

To crush thy calm defiance of his will.

The deep-drawn sighs of Briton's rugged sons

Responsive swell to Teuton's heart-wrung tears.

While flags, half-mast, droop o'er thy vanished years.

A soldier thou ! unblenching 'neath the guns ;

Not slaughter thy proud mission, but to save.

A mother's loving stay, a sister's pride,

Enshrouded lies in thy prime manhood's grave,

And mourning patients miss thee from their side.

Human ! farewell ! long be thy memory blest,

And soft thy bed on th' Great Physician's breast.

SONNET

To the Memory of E. H. Brown, a Brother Official.

———

DEATH'S cold imperious signal came to one
   Whose kindly presence cheered our common task
Through six long years.   With pleading sighs we ask
Is there, O Death, no grey-haired ling'rer ; none
Whose sere unhallowed life sheds seeds of ill,
   A fitter targe for thy relentless dart ?
   Spare, spare the ready hand, the loving heart,
The ringing voice whose tones we need to fill
The harmony of joyous song.   Behold
   The gentle wife and babes, with outstretched hands,—
The parents whom his filial arms enfold.
   All pleas are vain, as rain-drops on the sands,
But this we hear, " I strike at His behest
" Whose name is " Love ;" be sure that He knows best."

FOUR TAKEN AND FOUR LEFT.

In memory of four young ladies who were drowned while bathing in Algoa
Bay, Saturday 2nd October, 1886.

NO storm-battered bark in the midnight's deep gloom,
  Its hapless crew hurled on a surge-whitened coast ;
No world-weary women sought rest in a tomb
From poverty's struggles, or guilt's scowling ghost ;

But merrily sparkled the spray-crested wave,
That bore on its bosom a warrant to sweep,
Eight gay, laughing girls to a chill ocean grave,
Leaving their loved ones in anguish to weep.

Busy Death, as he gazed on so many bright eyes
In terror beholding his uplifted darts,
Relenting, abandoned the half of his prize,
And life again fluttered in four loving hearts.

Hand-in-hand dancing—the doomed and the saved—
They tread hand in-hand on Eternity's brink,—
Life and Death hand-in-hand ! O how we have craved
For light on these deeps where faint reasonings sink.

Our groping thought shrinks as it marks the wild waste
Of happy life given, and asks, " Was it well
To pluck tender blooms in such heart-crushing haste,
And rob earth of fragrance Heaven's raptures to swell?"

Peace, troubled soul ! " It is well with the child."
It is well with the saved—it is well with with the lost.
Leave riddles to gaze on His countenance mild,
Whose love has redeemed them at infinite cost.

113

HELP, LORD!

In memory of the REV. JOHN A. CHALMERS, Minister of the Presbyterian Church, Graham's Town, and the REV. JOHN C. MACINTOSH, Minister of the Congregational Church, Port Elizabeth.

"Help Lord, for the godly man ceaseth ; for the faithful fail from among the children of men." Ps. XII : I.

SLOWLY and silently mourners are sweeping,

With sorrow-veiled faces and garments of gloom,

While widows and fatherless children are weeping,

Along the drear pathway that leads to a tomb ;

Faint echoes, repeating the bell's solemn toll,

Seem to speak the hushed plaint of each grief-burdened soul,

"Help Lord " !

Help, Lord ! for the voice of the godly man ceaseth,

And the faithful ones fail from the children of men ;

Help, Lord ! for the kingdom of Satan increaseth,

And crowds throng the drunkard's and gambler's den ;

I

Help, Lord! for the light of the Gospel grows faint,
And Mammon's delights hide the crown of the saint.

" Help Lord " !

Help, Lord! for the Thy flag-bearers quickly are falling,
While faithless hearts fail in the battle with wrong ;
Help, Lord! for the grave's heedless summons is calling
The veterans who in the fight have grown strong ;
Help, Lord! for the shepherds in death are laid low,
And feeble sheep fall, 'neath the ravening foe.

" Help Lord " !

O not for the glorified, peacefully sleeping
In earth's kindly breast, are our silent tears shed,
But for those who in desolate dwellings are weeping
O'er the love and devotion entombed with the dead.
Two stars are withdrawn from our sin-clouded sight,
But their voices still ring, " Follow me to the light,"

" Help Lord " !

FAREWELL TO BATHURST.

D EAR beauteous spot, while I bid thee farewell
 A train of sad thoughts like a mountain stream's swell
Pour intomy soul, and the effort is vain
To repress its o'erflowings ; why need I refrain ?
Why long for his sordid insensible heart,
Who with spots so enchanting regretless can part,
Or his grovelling soul that ne'er glowed with delight
While gazing on scenes thus with loveliness bright.

Sweet Bathurst, I leave thee to mingle again
In the turmoil and cares that surround busy men ;
But thy vivid remembrance, congenial spot
Shall fondly be cherished whate'er be my lot.
Thy evergreen forests, thy verdure clad hills,
Thy kloofs and thy valleys, their torrents and rills,
Thy pastures luxuriant o'er studded with herds,
'Mong fragrant mimosa all vocal with birds,

Yon chaste lowly temple whose Sabbath day toll

Melodiously echoes from each grassy knoll,

Old ocean whose billows loud dashing on shore

The listening ear soothe with their far distant roar,

Each neat cheerful cottage where healthful delight

Where plenty and peace and contentment unite ;

These gardens and fields whose munificent soil

Rewards with exub'rance the labourer's toil :

The friends who with kindness none e'er can transcend

Frst welcomed the stranger nor ceased to befriend ;—

These all on mind's tablet a picture will form

In colours as fair as the bow 'mid the storm.

How oft when the toils of the day were gone by

And evening's gay gilding o'erflooded the sky,

When nature exulting in affluence dressed

Whispered peace to the mind by anxieties pressed,

Have I 'mong thy magical scenery strayed,

Sought flowers o'er the plain, or wild grapes in the glade,

Or leisurely roamed in the shady woods'maze

While the swelling heart gushed adoration and praise.

Or from yonder hill-top I have drank in the view—

The azure-robed mountains, the ocean's deep blue ;

Till entranced by the splendour that round me was poured,

My thoughts on the pinions of Fancy have soared

To those regions of bliss iron War never trod,

The viewless abode of fair nature's great God.

These halcyon hours are on mem'ry defined,

In characters deep and enduring as mind ;

In the retrospect view as ecstatic they'll seem

As if spent in some distant celestial dream ;

The thought of their joy a soft balm will impart

When cares and vexations embitter the heart ;

They'll appear in the visions by gay Fancy traced

Like verdant oases that grace the parched waste ;

Or like the Pacific's bright beauteous isles,

That gleam from the bosom of ocean with smiles.

Then why need I blush at the fall of a tear,

When parting with friends and attachments so dear ;

Or wherefore essay pensive feelings to quell

While I bid thee sweet Eden-like Bathurst, Farewell ?

BATHURST, 1847.

LEDBURY REVISITED JUNE 1884.

HAIL! scene endeared of budding childhood's days ;
    Old Time has touched thee with a gentle hand

Since, fifty years ago, I said farewell.

Time-worn and grey, I now with sober pace

Retread thy narrow streets and quaint old lanes,

And mark with clouded eyes familiar spots

Where troops of merry boys released from school

In contest keen pursued their noisy games.

Sadly I stroll around the hushed churchyard

Where heedless of their solemn calls to thought

We played at leap-frog o'er its mossy stones,

Or made its circuit in the eager race,

While life o'er brimmed in shouts and bounding glee.

Yonder the sylvan heights through which I roamed,

Climbing the trees in search of boy's delights:—

Birds nests and nuts, while saucy squirrels leaped

From bough to bough, and cuckoos piped their song.

There too the old familiar mansion stands

Retiring from the street, beneath whose roof

I conned my tasks, or drank in tranced delight

My gentle aunts' sweet strain from harp and song.

There too the rose-fringed winding garden walks

In which I chased my hoop or tired with play

I watched the gardener at his silent toil.

There, too, the belfry tower with sun-tipped spire

That heavenward points from dark umbrageous trees,

Whose giddy circling steps I panting climbed

To watch the ringers while they rang the chimes.

And there the grand old ivy-covered church

Whose deep-arched door I entered sad and slow

With hushed and trembling awe, led by the hand,

A tiny mourner at my father's grave—

The solemn scene seems but as yesterday

So deep the impress of my first great grief.

And now as mem'ry travels up the course

Of those long years and pauses here and there

At well-marked mile-stones on the devious way,

What varied pictures she displays to view.

What joys and griefs, what victories and defeats,

What light and cloud alternate mark the scene ;

What strivings after good, what driftings down,

What noble aspirations unattained,

What galling wrongs that crushed all hope and joy,

What gentle kindnesses that cheered the road

And filled the heart with grateful memories

That rise as odours from a bed of flowers ;

   While here mid scenes of richest lovliness

And tender visions of my distant home

This retrospect I take, a Father's hand

I trace in all the way.   O may He still

My guide and succour be, and what remains

To me of life in sorrow or in joy

Be humbly dedicated to His praise.

LEDBURY, HEREFORDSHIRE, 1884.

THE BEES.—A FABLE.

On the proposal to separate the Eastern and Western Provinces of the Cape of Good Hope.

SPIRIT that once old Æsop fired,
    Lend me thine aid that I, inspired
By his mysterious lore, may know
(What learned Burritt ne'er could show),
The language of each sentient thing,
The thoughts that in its bosom spring ;
That we from all may wisdom learn
The path of safety to discern.
    In an old barrel 'twixt two trees
Resided once a swarm of bees ;
Beneath one queen's benignant sway,
They laboured on from day to day,
While flowers were blooming, weather sunny,
To store their hive with choicest honey.

No quarrel e'er disturbed their rest

Each helped his brother when distressed,

While thus they lived they never failed

To conquer whate'er foe assailed.

I almost had forget to tell

(What everybody knows full well),

Their wooden dwelling had two doors

And so adjusted were their stores

Contiguous to these entrances

That into two assemblages

(Alas ! that it should be so fated)

They partially were separated ;

Hence we will term them if you please

The bung-hole and the spigot bees.

 Long might this happy family

Have lived in blissful harmony,

But so it happ'd some rainy weather

Kept them at home long time together, ;

In spring-time too when as we know

Their honey yet was rather low.

At length complaints waxed energetic

For, fasting long, they grew splenetic

And wanting better occupation

Began a noisy declamation

Upon the troubles of the nation.

The bung-hole bees discussed taxation,

But kept in bounds of moderation,

The spigot bees grew much more heated

And vowed they of their rights were cheated ;

Their distant Queen came seldom near 'em

With delicacies sweet to cheer 'em.

One orator, a wise old saw,

Harangued them on the Salic law ;

So forcibly he pointed out

That on their minds he left no doubt

That all their grievances and woes

From female tyranny arose,

Thenceforth their thoughts were fully bent
Upon a separate government.

    Long time it took them to determine
Whom they should now enrobe in ermine,
The merits of each insect creature
Its habits, tastes, its form and feature,
Were long discussed with erudition
By many a new-made politician.
At length they pitched upon the hornet
To rule the kingdom and adorn it,
And after stormy declamation
They named a formal deputation
To wait upon him, first fine day
And hear what he would deign to say.

    The sun shone forth and off they pressed
To find the wily hornet's nest ;
He met them with great condescension,
Heard their request with calm attention,

Said he regretted such dissension

But since it was their firm intention

To be an independent nation

He would accept their invitation.

He soon arrived, with acclamation,

At night a grand illumination,

Three golden bands—his decoration—

Struck all with greatest admiration ;

He in their eyes was all perfection—

He would ensure them safe protection.

    While summer held all were content

With their new form of government,

But winter came and with it brought

Trouble of which they had not thought.

Their king demanded to sustain him

So much that they could not maintain him.

His strings of uncles, nephews, cousins

And hangers-on in hungry dozens

Alas ! had eaten all their store

Ere yet the winter was half o'er.

Now dismal cupboard-bare starvation

Alarmed this independent nation ;

Their king from hunger was half dead

And dismal drooped each courtier's head.

To add to their forlorn dismay

Some huge black ants made an essay

Of all they had to take possession,

Well knowing their infirm condition.

Too weak to stand in stern resistance

They sent a drone to beg assistance

Of their kind friends the bung-hole bees,

If 'twere not granted would they please

To lend their state a little honey !

The bung-bees thought it wondrous funny ;

They laughed until the hive resounded

At such request, till quite confounded

The drone in hopeless plight returned

And told his tale ; each bosom burned

With hot revenge and indignation

At such contempt for their great nation.

They struggled long against their fate,

But saw their folly when too late.

The ants expelled them all from home

And took possession of their comb.

The moral with my bow I leave

To Eastern folk who won't believe

'Tis best to let what's well alone

At least until we've stronger grown.

GRAHAM'S TOWN,
1849.

SCRIP.

THERE'S nothing like scrip,
　　When you've got the straight tip,
For winning a smile from your banker ;
　　By "bulling" and " bearing,"
　　With caution and daring,
You grow fat while your gudgeons grow lanker.

　　The virtues that lurk
　　In an honest day's work
Are moonshine to shares in a gold mine ;
　　Hey ! Presto ! you're up,
　　Holding Fortune's full cup,
While dolts stand agape at your bold line.

　　Economize truth,
　　And let no feeble ruth
Pipe her eye o'er the fall of a gaby ;
　　Look well to your broker—
　　If conscience speaks, choke her—
And take care that you don't "hold the baby."

K

THE LOSS OF THE SIX HUNDRED

(With apologies to Lord Tennyson).

———

HALF-A-CROWN!   Half-a-crown!
    Every rap plundered ;
All my dear Granny left,
    Sovereigns, six hundred.
Forward ! the broker said,
Into the " swim " he led,
Soon, winged by scrip, there fled,
    Three of six hundred.

Forward ! the broker cried,
Flowing is Fortune's tide ;
Hope and be undismayed
    Though you have blundered.
Mine not to make reply,
Mine not to reason why,
Mine but to sign and sigh
    O'er all my six hundred.

When will my Div's be paid ?

O what wild fibs were made

While schemers planned their raid ;

    E'en Satan wondered.

Bright visions all are flown ;

From Granny's cold head-stone

Hear a deep reproachful groan

    O'er her six hundred.

THE BEETLE AND THE BEE.

A Fable for the Young.

WITH nose in the gravel, and heels in the air,
 A wheelbarrow beetle slow tumbled
A huge ball of rubbish he scarcely knew where,
 As backwards, blindfolded, he fumbled.

"Whither go you, good sir?" quoth a gay honey bee
 Looking down from a sweet-laden flower.
"Your treasure is bulky, whatever it be,
 And I fear it o'ertaxes your power,"

The beetle collected his sorely-tried legs,
 And wiped the great drops from his forehead.
"'Tis big," he replied, "but it holds all my eggs
 As well as a lot that I've borrowed."

" Yon hillock will furnish some suitable mould
    For storing my coveted treasure.
When my family's fledged you'll be ' out in the cold '
    While we're flying on pinions of pleasure."

Thus churlishly boasting, his task he resumed,
    Still backward his bundle propelling,
Unwitting, alas ! of the danger that loomed,
    While vainglory his bosom was swelling.

The best devised projects of beetles and men
    (As the Scottish bard long ago taught us)
Go often astray, since our shortsighted ken
    Sees but few of the ills that may thwart us.

By pushing and kicking, with toil unremitting,
    At length he attained the mound's summit,
When, lo ! o'er the margin his bundle goes flitting
    Down a deep yawning pit like a plummet.

As the bee, honey-laden, his homeward way sped
 He saw the poor beetle distracted,
 His vaunting voice silenced, his gay visions fled,
 His legs, with sore labour, contracted.

And as he buzzed onward this moral he pondered :
 " Don't put all your eggs in one bundle.
If you'd avoid sorrow, don't recklessly borrow,
 And look well ahead when you trundle."

SOUTH AFRICAN JUBILEE ODE.

FROM wild Zambezi's roaring falls
 To Table Bay's grim castle walls
Old Afric swells thy loud acclaim
 Victoria our Queen !
Whose honoured name lights Britain's fame
 With virtue's silver sheen.
Queen of England brave and free,
Guard of sacred liberty,
With loyal hearts and bended knee
We hail thy gladsome Jubilee !

Basuto, Kafir, Bechuan,
And wild-waifs from each roving clan
On answering hill tops pæans raise
 To thy deserved renown.
Britons and Dutch united praise
 The halo round thy crown.

Queen of England brave and free,

Hand-clasped we swear true fealty,

With loyal hearts and bended knee

We hail thy gladsome Jubilee !

No hireling bayonets fence thy throne,

Thy towers no regal captives own ;

No need hast thou of lurking spies,

But woe to him who rears

The torch of treason, and defies

Affection's clustered spears.

Queen of England brave and free,

Should foes assail, we offer thee

Our noblest blood, while loyally

We hail thy gladsome Jubilee !

While lofty bards thy glories sing,

Our hearts their fondest tendrils fling

Around thee for the virtues calm

    That grace thy genial sway.

We bless thee for thy kindly balm

    In sorrow's dreary day.

Queen of England brave and free,

Fount of loving sympathy,

With loyal hearts and bended knee

We hail thy gladsome Jubilee!

Great King of kings! our prayer we raise,—

May richest blessings crown her days,—

Let guardian seraphs from above

    Defend our noble Queen.

May Justice, Mercy, Truth, and Love,

    Aye keep her laurels green.

And when at that imperious call,

Which comes in Thy good time to all,

She lays the well-borne sceptre down,

And yields her earthly diadem,

138

May he who wore a thorny crown

Bedeck her brow with a peerless gem

Of never fading sheen.

Queen of England brave and free,

Heaven's best gifts we ask for thee,

With bended heads right reverently,

On this thy gladsome Jubilee !

Copies of " this Jubilee Ode" were graciously accepted and acknowledged by Her Majesty the Queen and His Excellency Sir Hercules Robinson, the Governor of the Colony.

FAREWELL TO FIFTY-FIVE.

FAREWELL, farewell old Fifty-five ! to thee,
This circling ball no longer homage yields :
Thy record 's closed, and frail humanity
Stands trembling 'neath the rod that conscience wields.
For now methinks, that record's page reveals
A long dark roll of follies, faults, and crimes
Before His eye, whose love in vain appeals
To hearts ingrate ; whose goodness glads our times,
And spreads with genial gifts the wide earth's varied
climes.

Upon thy winged hours old Fifty-five
Alternate hopes and fears have trembling hung,
Capricious as the fleecy clouds which drive
Athwart the summer sky, a motley throng
Of joys, and griefs, have swiftly swept along.

Now o'er the welkin peal the bridal bells ;

   Anon the mournful funeral dirge is sung ;

Big with this truth each passing moment swells,—

   " Beyond the sky alone unchanging pleasure dwells."

   Farewell old Fifty-five ! the visions fair

Which down thy sparkling vista erst appeared,

   Beguiling Mammon's votaries with the glare

Of sordid wealth in pile on pile upreared.

   Have flitted past, and left a blank uncheered,

By one bright gleam, in many an aching breast [1]

   O were the sober truth more wide revered,

And gaping folly's golden dreams repressed,

   How few would groan beneath the gambler's dark unrest.

   Few were our tears, old Fifty-five, hadst thou

Consigned alone the noisome vampire band

   To disappointment blank, and carking woe ;

---

[1]. Great speculation took place this year in Namaqualand Copper Mining Shares which resulted in the ruin of a large number of incautious speculators.

But thou with undiscriminating hand

    Has flung on poverty's inclement strand

Full many a one styled "noblest work of God."

    His lowing herds have perished from the land, [1]

Or haply o'er his fields a blight has trod ;

    Still, *he* can trusting say " My father holds the rod."

    Farewell old Fifty-five ! bright o'er thy days.

Celestial Truth has flung her radiant bow ;

    Benignant from her throne she stoops to raise

Each moiling slave of ignorance and woe.

    Her silv'ry voice proclaims to high and low

This blood bought word, " man's mind and tongue are free."

    May ev'ry human breast responsive glow,

Till superstition, pride, and bigotry,

    Their lofty heads abase, and like grim spectres flee.

---

[1] The " lung-sickness " among cattle first appeared in a virulent form this year, carrying off vast numbers. This trouble was intensified by a very severe drought.

Farewell old Fifty-five ! inhuman War

With blood-red hand has o'er thy cycle swept.

   Horrific still he rolls his thund'ring car

'Mid ghastly wounds, and dying groans unwept

   The cannon's roar which long in silence slept,

Unceasing echoes o'er the dismal scene ;

   Deep blushing, Mercy from her throne has stept,

While eager Rapine stalks with hideous mien,

   And gloating scans the flaming city's lurid sheen. [1]

   O Liberty ! Britannia's proudest boast ;

O Liberty ! man's brightest heritage ;

   Why on thy steps attendant should a host

Of sanguinary passions fiercely rage ?

   Or why should hist'ry's memorable page

Be blotted o'er with sighs and groans and tears ?

   When will grey time mature the golden age,

When men shall snap their swords and quiv'ring spears,

   And Peace triumphant reign o'er all the circling years ?

Farewell old Fifty-five—as ling'ring still

Thy last faint echoes on the ear expire,

   And sadd'ning thoughts the heaving bosom fill

Hope strings anew her animating lyre.

   Eternal truth—the soul's immortal fire—

Ere long shall claim the homage of the world,

   High o'er gaunt Slav'ry's blazing funeral pyre

Shall Freedom's crimson banner wave unfurl'd,

   And Ignorance and Vice from their dark thrones be hurl'd.

---

[1] The Crimean war and the destruction of Sevastopol.

1886-87.

"So teach us to number our days that we may apply our hearts
unto wisdom." Ps. 90 : 12.

THE ponderous pendulum of time
Marks off the years with ruthless swing ;
The passing bells swell loud their chime
While eighty-six takes ghostly wing.

Like shadows on the mountain side,
Its moments, days, and months, have fled ;
And wreckage left by an ebbing tide
Fit emblem shows of its vain hopes dead.

Gone are its joys, its sorrows sleep ;
Its record's sealed of good and ill,
Till resurrection light shall leap.
And all before the throne stand still.

Beyond recall its works and ways ;

Beyond recall its thoughts and words ;

To requiems sad o'er wasted days

The past returns no answering chords.

Then "let the dead past bury its dead :"

Hope forward springs with cheering voice ;

Our future steps by wisdom led

Mid fragrant blossems may rejoice.

Let high resolve for noble fight

With foes that bar our way to heaven,

And purpose firm to do the right

Hallow the dawning eighty-seven.

Lord ! we are weak, but Thou art strong ;

With bended heads we ask Thine ai l ;

Light Thou our way—raise Thou our song

Till hopes in glad fruition fade.

L

WELCOME TO 1887.

GOOD wishes ! good wishes for young eighty-seven !

    Away with the vanished year's spiritless leaven.

        With high hopes and aims,

        Let us peg out our claims

On the bountiful field for new enterprize given.

Gaily the budding year steps to her throne,

Her flowing locks decked with a glistening crown,

        And round her a throng,

        Rough, cheery, and strong,

Of miners who've marked golden ingots their own.

Success to the diggers in heart-leaping measure :

'(May they delve not unmindful of better " hid treasure") ;

        May hard honest labour,

        Find Fortune's fair favour,

And the riches of rocks roll rivers of pleasure.

May sweeping clouds empty their life giving rain
O'er hills and dales smiling with generous grain ;

    May sleek flocks and herds,

    And fine feathered " birds,"

The farmers heart gladden with o'erflowing gain.

May brotherhood flourish, and each lend a hand
To spread light and happiness far through the land ;

    May the clear lamp of knowledge

    From Church, School, and College,

Put Error to flight with her withering brand.

May the mantle of Peace spread wide o'er our ball,
And sword bristling empires in dark ruin fall.

    No tyranny chaining,

    In our streets no complaining ;

May grateful hearts swell to the Giver of all.

TO REV. J. D. ROBINSON, M.A.

WITH M.S. COPIES OF SOUTH AFRICAN POEMS, ON HIS LEAVING
PORT ELIZABETH.

———

MY timorous muse in awe of the scorner
   With drooping wings sat up in a corner ;
But hearing a kindly word from you
She smoothed her pinions and out she flew
      To take an evening airing.
   The Empyrean she tried
   But her fainting song died
On a flight too presumptiously daring ;
   So she toppled to earth
   With shrunk faith in her worth
And relinquished her dignified bearing.
But as she scrambled home again
'Mid manifold stumbles and trippings
That her jaunt should not be quite in vain
She gathered a few Cape clippings

Which with diffident blushes she here presents

For your kindly acceptance with compliments.

And with ardent good wishes she closes her song

To which our hearts echo in sympathy strong ;

That in health, wealth, and peace your days may be long ;

That your sword may flash bright in the battle with wrong,

And the soul-stirring power of your eloquent tongue

Add many glad harps to the star-spangled throng.

TO GRAAFF-REINET.

———

HAIL! gem of the desert in slumber reposing
    The dark hills thy cradle, soft verdure thy bed
The breeze from the kloof richest perfumes disclosing
Lightly sweeps o'er thy bosom raising dust very red.

The last gleams of the sun in gray splendour descending
Seem fondly to linger around the tall spire
While the clouds rainbow-tinted their gorgeous hues lending
Make the Dutchmen's black chimneys seems as if all afire.

Deep-bosomed in shade the dark river meanders
Save where like a mirror it gleams from the glade
Or soapy and slimy through mud-holes it wanders
Where stockings are washed by a Hottentot maid.

Sweet abode of content! dearly loved Graaff-Reinet!
Long, long mayst thou bask in thy slumber profound
Tame spring-bucks be baited for a six-penny bet
And thy butter be sold at four shillings per pound.

THE LAMENT OF THE DONKIN STREET STREAMLET,

On being Entombed by an Unpoetical Municipality.

O LIST good folks a tale of woe
    A tale of dark oppression ;
Let briny tears your cheeks down flow
In sorrowful procession.

Till late I trickled down the glen
In sunbeams gaily sparkling ;
But now entombed by heartless men
I creep on cold and darkling.

Beneath a huge chaotic mass
Of rubbish vile I mutter ;
'Mid frogs and fungi rank alas
A melancholy gutter.

No more my bosom decked with green
Relieves the eye aweary ;
Its verdant slopes no more are seen
But all around is dreary,

No more the breeze with fitful sigh
Along my bed breathes mildly ;
No more when Boreas blusters high
My caverns echo wildly.

The rustic bridge that bound my banks
In brotherhood together
Is torn away and its rude planks
Are gone, the "Board" knows whither

Away ! a dire revenge I'll brew
My rage meanwhile I'll bung tight
That sordid Board the day shall rue
When next I see the sunlight.

When turbid torrents rushing pass
Adown my peeping square holes,
Right through this execrable mass
I mad-man like will tear holes.

I'll heave aloft this lumb'ring load
And crashing down I'll toss it
Till in the middle of the road
A mountain I deposit.

Port Elizabeth, 1854.

THE SONG OF THE LAMP LIGHTER, WITH CHORUS.

YE men of "light and leading,"
 Town Councillors and such,
O hear the lamp-posts pleading
 For the lighter's cheery touch.
  The Liverpool of Africa
   Has reached a sorry pass
  When country cousins laugh, " ha ! ha !
   " Yer can't pay fur yer gas."

We have a spacious market
 (Cost fifty thousand pounds) :
But through the hollow dark it
 Repeats these doleful sounds ;
  The Liverpool of Africa
   Has reached a sorry pass
  For ostrich spectres laugh, " ha ! ha !
   " Yer can't pay fur yer gas."

Each thievish loafer prowling

Deems it a jolly lark

To keep Bayonians growling

O'er pillage in the dark.

The Liverpool of Africa

Has reached a sorry pass

When ragged rascals laugh, " ha ! ha !

" Yer can't pay fur yer gas."

Note.—At the time I now write the lamps are alight.

A PETITION TO THE MAYOR OF PORT ELIZABETH.

ᴹY dear Mr. Mayor
    Lend an ear to the prayer
Of a martyr to chronic lumbago ;
  Let your pitying soul her
  Sighs pour o'er my dolour,
  And grant that your roller
On White's Road a smoothing tour may go.

  I am sorry to trouble ye,
  But that road is so " nubbly"
That the jolts of a cab are quite awful ;
  From the Square to " The Grand"
  Only stern self-command
  (Not always at hand)
Can stopper down language unlawful.

Let Perkin'-street slide,

And soft Green-street abide

It's turn for your road-mending band ;

Be this the first work you seize

My spine-cracking jerks to ease

Send snorting " Sir Hercules" *

On the road that leads up to " The Grand."

*The steam roller is so named.

POOR JANE JAMIESON.

"A poor young woman, named Jane Jamieson, was found this morning by Constable Weir, in Murray's Lane, in a very destitute condition, her only covering being a few gunny bags. As she was very sick, the constable removed her to the lock-up to await the inspection of the district surgeon." *E. P. Herald. June* 18.

SICK, sore, and deserted mid squalor and rags,
  Jane Jamieson lies in a dark fœtid lane ;
And beneath a cold cover of coarse gunny bags,
  She hopelessly tosses in fever and pain.
              What matters ?
          "The town has nothing to do with it."

Who knocks at the door ?—'Tis the Constable Weir,
  Who while walking his rounds has "permiscously " found
    her,
And brushing away a Scotch constable's tear,
  He gathers his brother policemen around her.
              What matters ?
          "The town has nothing to do with it."

As the sun blazes forth on the gay gladsome earth,

    And mockingly gleams from the sky-pointing spire,

They bear their sad burden, of so little worth,

    To the jail, where Bay charity fans her small fire.

            What matters?

              "The town has nothing to do with it."

Port Elizabeth has since obliterated all cause for the reproach conveyed in the above lines, She has now a large and well conducted Hospital where unfortunates like " Jane Jamieson " receive every possible kindness and attention.

WOMAN'S LOVE.

—

WHAT lights on beauteous infant face
    The radiant smile of joy;
What in that smile essays to trace
    The reason's first employ?
        'Tis woman's love.

When toddling footsteps trip and fail
    Or tears proclaim a smart
What soothes the pain and tells a tale
    Till sleep its balms impart?
        Tis woman's love.

When heedless youth with ardent soul
    Speeds folly's downward track
What meekly points the fatal goal
    And gently leads him back?
        A woman's love

When youth to manhood yields the place

    What then I ask inspires

His selfish heart with gen'rous grace

    And wakes its noblest fires

        Like woman's love ?

When chill adversity's dark waves

    Roll o'er the hapless head

What's the uplifting hand that saves

    Amid those billows dread ?

        'Tis woman's love.

When life's flood flows out chillingly

    And anguish lays us low

Who in that hour would willingly

    The sacred proofs forego

        Of woman's love ?

When health and peace our path o'erstrew
  With fragrance-breathing flowers
What is the softly-falling dew
  That heightens all their powers?
    'Tis woman's love

Like some glad verdure-spreading stream
  Fed by exhaustless springs,
Or like the sun whose cheering beam
  Adorns all earthly things
    Is woman's love.

SONG.—ALONE

WHEN Luna pours her silv'ry light
O'er Nature's peaceful face
And sheds upon the silent night
A soul-subduing grace ;
I love to be alone
Alone, alone
I love to be alone.

When on some cliff erect and rude
I list the waves' wild roar ;
Or slowly stray in pensive mood
Along the pebbled shore
'Tis sweet to be alone ;
Alone, alone
'Tis sweet to be alone.

Amid the forests' tangled maze

    Beside the limpid stream

Far from the world's unfeeling gaze

    Enrapt in Fancy's dream

        O let me be alone

          Alone, alone

        O let me be alone.

But where, O where, would be the charm

    In forest, rock or dell,

Had I no friend with bosom warm

    To listen while I tell

        My bliss while I'm alone?

        Alone, alone

        My bliss while I'm alone.

GLEE FOR ARBOR DAY.

AIR, " *The Chough and Crow.*"

THE stripling pine and tiny oak
    Extol, in merry tune,
Harmonious with the young school folk,
    The twenty-fifth of June.
Like lambkins leaping from their pen
    In freedom we shall play ;
Uprouse ye then, ye little maids and men,
    It is our Arbor Day.

              Chorus : Uprouse ye then, &c

For we shall grow while you're asleep,
    And wave our branches high ;
We'll strike our roots to fountains deep,
    And woo the cloud-clad sky.

Our verdure bright to grateful ken

    Will bounteous charms display ;

Uprouse ye then, ye little maids and men.

    It is our Arbor Day.

                Chorus : Uprouse ye then, &c.

The wild vine green and clematis

    Will twine with tendril tongue ;

While gentle bush-doves coo their bliss

    And feed their callow young.

The humble bee from leafy den

    Will hum his soothing lay

Uprouse ye then, ye little maids and men,

    It is our Arbor Day.

                Chorus : Uprouse ye then, &c.

But tend us well with loving care,

    Nor let ill weeds annoy,

Till sturdy strength life's storms to bear

    Ensures our future joy.

Our shimmering shade o'er hill and glen

 Will all your care repay ;

Uprouse ye then, ye little maids and men,

 It is our Arbor Day.

     Chorus : Uprouse ye then, &c.

SONNET.

.

To Lewis Morris, M.A., Author of " Songs of Two Worlds,"
" The Ode of Life," &c.

FROM distant clime, sweet singer I invoke

The spirit of thy song, and hail thy lyre

A heaven-strung gift from yonder angel choir

To cheer sad **Toilers** 'neath an earth-clogged yoke.

The melody of thy mellifluous lines

Reverb'rates from the conscious strings that bind

" Two worlds " in one ; sky-climbing thoughts, entwined

With feeling, spring from thy rich page, like pines

From verdant mountain slope.   O! for the power

To catch from **Albion's** hills the echoes sweet

Of thy full tones, and Afric's wilds to shower

With strains responsive, such as thou wilt greet ;

Halting and faint mayhap, yet blending true

With life's great psalm resounding ever new.

The author having sent to Lewis Morris copies of some of the poems in this collection was favoured with a most kind and encouraging acknowledgment from which he ventures to quote the following extract " I have read your poems with great pleasure and I hope you will continue to express yourself in verse, the tone of which leaves nothing to be desired and the literary merits of which are so considerable. It is one of the justest pleasures of a literary life, exposed as it is to much unfair and unworthy criticism that it brings a writer into connexion with those who though they are far removed from him in space are yet bound to him by the closest ties of common sympathy and common aspirations after good."

THE FAITHFUL FRIEND.

A LITTLE dog, who missed the kindly care
  Of one who long since had been laid to rest,
Sought out his master's vacant office chair,
  And waiting, hushed the sorrows of his breast.

Poor faithful dog! In sympathetic grief
  I mourn with thee thy much-loved master's loss,
But Hope, whose cordial pours for thy relief,
  Sheds no sweet drop to ease my cheerless cross.

Wait on poor dog; I would not if I could
  Dispel the dream that lights thy wonted bed;
Thy visions fair of romps in merry mood,
  Wound up with gentle pats upon thy head.

I love the trust that in the far-off land

Our faithful dogs will bear us company,

The home that gathers all the loyal band

Will surely have " sweet fields " for such as thee.

The subject of the above lines was a small terrier belonging to my de-
parted friend and fellow official, E. H. Brown. The little animal had quite
passed out of mind until he suddenly appeared and coiled himself up in his
accustomed place many months after the decease of his master.

VOICES OF THE SEA.

O MYSTIC-VOICED, immeasurable sea !
   Thought cowers in sight of thine immensity :
   To thy chill depths profound
Man's tiny plummet stretches wavering down.
Only to write them fathomless, unknown,
   In primal silence bound.

O solemn-voiced, immeasurable sea !
Thy ceaseless surge bespeaks Eternity ;
   The sand grains on thy shore,—
The numbered drops that fill thy brimming cup
Are steps by which dull thought still labours up
   To grasp the " Evermore."

O thunder-voiced, immeasurable sea !
Thy storms sweep forth in dread sublimity ;
   And 'neath their swirling rage

Man's steel-ribbed monuments are crushed like shells,

And thy green wave with sullen grandeur tells

    Of a dirgeless, death-writ page.

O order-voiced, immeasurable sea !

Thy floods are bounded by a firm decree,

    And in God's hollow hand

Thy rolling waves obedient rise or fall,

To lift the beauteous islands of our ball

    Or whelm its desert sand.

O angel-voiced, immeasurable sea !

Thy calm expanse breathes sweet tranquillity ;

    When moonlight's tender ray

In glistening glory streams athwart thy breast,

Thou shewest a pictured pathway to the rest

    That ends the Christian's day.

THE WHISPERING PINE.

THE Lordly Poet's ' Talking Oak"
    Is not the only tree
Whose voice has waked the rhyming folk
    To answering minstrelsy.

Up-springing from a neighbouring street
    A Norfolk Island Pine,
My morning fancy seems to greet,
    With whisperings divine.

And well I wot that heavenly lore,
    Streams from all things below,
To hearts whose peaceful waters pour
    With sympathetic flow.

The Tennysonian talking tree,
    Discoursed of earthly love ;
Yon dear old pine-tree talks to me
    In thoughts that soar above.

It towers beyond the chimmey tops
  In scorn of nether things ;
It needs no cumbrous earthly props
  As to and fro it swings.

Its stem elastic, tapering, high,
  Like some tall frigate's mast,
Defined against the azure sky,
  Rejoices in the blast.

In jutting whorls its branches spread,
  With equal space between
Each higher whorl with minished bed
  To its tiny top of green.

While just below the point, sky-capped,
  Its latest branchlets peer,
And form a little cross, enwrapt
  With memories sweet and clear.

I dare not blame those pious souls
    Whose meek devotions sink
To a brazen cross, while incense rolls
    And tapers dimly blink.

But more I prize the little cross
    Which greets my waking sight,
Above the clouds that chimneys toss
    Bedecked with heaven's own light.

On either hand a tall spire gleams
    Straight pointing to the sky ;
Each worshipper beneath them deems
    His neighbour's spire awry.

Up-piled by erring human hands
    No heaven-sent breezes sway,
Defiant, rigid, each one stands,
    No life nor growth have they.

Like yon fair tree, root-firm yet free,

   May I unwearied climb ;

And as each whorl marks out for me

   The yearly flight of time,

With growing light life's heights ascend,

   Each span with wider view,

Till striving years shall skyward end

   Cross-crowned in regions new.

www.ingramcontent.com/pod-product-compliance
Lightning Source LLC
Chambersburg PA
CBHW030606040726
47497CB00008B/2865